Math

GRADE 4

BRIGHTER CHILD®

Table of Contents

Brighter Child®
An imprint of Carson-Dellosa Publishing LLC
P.O. Box 35665
Greensboro, NC 27425 USA

Printed in Minster, OH USA • All rights reserved.   ISBN 0-7696-7614-6

4 5 6 7 8 9 10 GLO 14 13 12 11 10   252107784

Place Value

Place value is the value of a digit, or numeral, shown by where it is in the number. For example, in 1,234, **1** has the place value of thousands, **2** is hundreds, **3** is tens, and **4** is ones.

Directions: Write the numbers in the correct boxes to find how far the car has traveled.

one thousand
six hundreds
eight ones
nine ten thousands
four tens
two millions
five hundred thousands

millions	hundred thousands	ten thousands	thousands	hundreds	tens	ones
,			,			

How many miles has the car traveled?_____

Directions: In the number . . .

2,386   _____   is in the ones place.

4,957   _____   is in the hundreds place.

102,432   _____   is in the ten thousands place.

489,753   _____   is in the thousands place.

1,743,998   _____   is in the millions place.

9,301,671   _____   is in the hundred thousands place.

7,521,834   _____   is in the tens place.

Place Value: Expanded Notation and Standard Form

Directions: Use the number cube or spinner to create numbers for the place value boxes below. Then, write the number in expanded notation and standard form.

Example:

thousands	hundreds	tens	ones
8	6	2	4

Standard Form ___8,624___

Expanded Notation ___8,000 + 600 + 20 + 4___

thousands	hundreds	tens	ones

Standard Form _____

Expanded Notation _____

ten thousands	thousands	hundreds	tens	ones

Standard Form _____

Expanded Notation _____

hundred thousands	ten thousands	thousands	hundreds	tens	ones

Standard Form _____

Expanded Notation _____

Directions: Write the value of the **4** in each number below.

742,521 _____

456 _____

1,234,567 _____

65,504 _____

937,641 _____

Addition

4 → Find the ▓▓ 4 -row.

+ 5 → Find the 5 -column.

9 ← The sum is named where the
4-row and 5-column meet.

Use the table to add.

$$\begin{array}{r} 7 \\ + 8 \\ \hline \end{array}$$

5-column

+	0	1	2	3	4	5	6	7	8	9
0	0	1	2	3	4	5	6	7	8	9
1	1	2	3	4	5	6	7	8	9	10
2	2	3	4	5	6	7	8	9	10	11
3	3	4	5	6	7	8	9	10	11	12
4	4	5	6	7	8	9	10	11	12	13
5	5	6	7	8	9	10	11	12	13	14
6	6	7	8	9	10	11	12	13	14	15
7	7	8	9	10	11	12	13	14	15	16
8	8	9	10	11	12	13	14	15	16	17
9	9	10	11	12	13	14	15	16	17	18

4-row

Directions: Add.

5 +3	2 +5	5 +4	6 +3	3 +4	3 +5	2 +7	3 +7
6 +2	3 +6	3 +2	2 +4	4 +3	2 +6	7 +2	4 +4
2 +3	0 +7	3 +1	9 +0	1 +8	0 +5	4 +2	6 +1
7 +9	6 +7	9 +4	8 +3	4 +9	7 +3	8 +5	8 +9
7 +7	9 +5	4 +7	6 +5	2 +8	7 +5	4 +8	7 +6
9 +6	5 +8	5 +9	6 +6	9 +8	7 +4	3 +9	2 +9
4 +6	1 +9	5 +7	9 +3	3 +8	8 +4	9 +7	9 +9

Leafy Addition

Directions: Add, then color according to the code.

Code:

green — 79	orange — 35	red — 78
yellow — 87	purple — 56	brown — 94

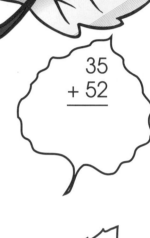

$$57 + 21$$

$$34 + 22$$

$$23 + 12$$

$$35 + 52$$

$$15 + 41$$

$$62 + 32$$

$$20 + 74$$

$$34 + 44$$

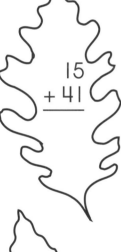

$$56 + 23$$

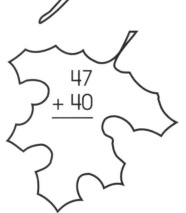

$$47 + 40$$

$$27 + 8$$

$$63 + 16$$

Math: Grade 4

Adding Larger Numbers

When adding two-, three-, and four-digit numbers, add the ones first, then tens, hundreds, thousands, and so on.

Examples:

Tens	Ones
5	4
+ 2	5
	9

Tens	Ones
5	4
+ 2	5
7	9

Directions: Add the following numbers.

81	67	34	730
+23	+22	+82	+265

76	1,803	523	267
+73	+1,104	+476	+ 12

		4,254	111
		+ 545	+ 82

		164	727
		+425	+ 51

8

Subtraction

Subtraction is "taking away" or subtracting one number from another.

Directions: Complete the following problems as quickly and as accurately as you can.

18 − 9	13 − 6	12 − 5	17 − 8	16 − 8
12 − 5	10 − 4	5 − 3	14 − 6	15 − 9
9 −5	8 − 3	6 − 2	5 − 4	10 − 7
11 − 4	12 − 8	16 − 9	11 − 8	10 −10

How quickly did you complete this page? _____

Subtraction: Regrouping

Directions: Subtract using regrouping.

Examples:

```
       1
 23    2 3
-18   - 1 8
        5
```

```
          1 13
 243    2 4 3
- 96   -  9 6
        1 4 7
```

```
  81        76        94       156       341       726
- 53      - 49      - 38      -  77     -  83      -  29
```

```
 568       806       743       903       647       254
-173      -738      -550      -336      -289      -  69
```

```
 730       961       573       604       265       372
-518      -846      -  76     -  55     -  19     -  59
```

```
 111       358       147
-  82     -  99     -  49
```

```
 180       325       873
-106      -  68     -  35
```

Addition and Subtraction

Directions: Add or subtract, using regrouping when needed.

```
   32          183          456
   68          246          398          643
 + 43        +  89        + 597        - 377
```

```
 1,563        3,586        8,711        9,361
 -  941      + 4,218      - 4,937      - 7,452
```

```
                293
                431          743          250
 5,734        +  93        - 529        +  82
+ 6,298       
```

```
 1,227
 2,431        9,117
+ 5,792      - 3,828
```

68 + 93 + 146 = _____   73 + 246 + 1,579 = _____

43 + 745 – 29 = _____   128 + 403 + 2,571 = _____

156 + 627 + 541 = _____   97 + 51 + 37 + 79 = _____

Tom walks 389 steps from his house to the video store. It is 149 steps to Elm Street. It is 52 steps from Maple Street to the video store. How many steps is it from Elm Street to Maple Street? _____

         Math: Grade 4

Name _____

Rounding: Tens

Rounding a number means expressing it to the nearest ten, hundred, thousand, and so on. Knowing how to round numbers makes estimating sums, differences, and products easier. When rounding to the nearest ten, the key number is in the ones place. If the ones digit is **5** or larger, round up to the next highest ten. If the ones digit is **4** or less, round down to the nearest ten.

Examples:
- Round 81 to the nearest ten.
- **1** is the key digit.
- If it is less than **5**, round down.
- Answer: <u>80</u>
- Round 246 to the nearest ten.
- **6** is the key digit.
- If it is more than **5**, round up.
- Answer: <u>250</u>

Directions: Round these numbers to the nearest ten.

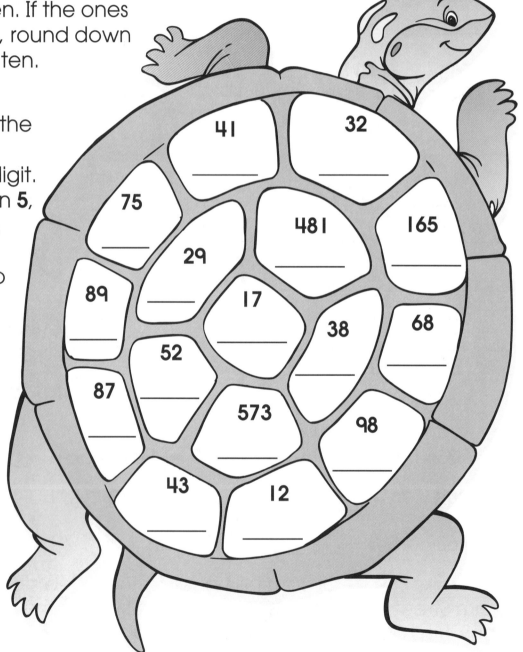

Name _____

Rounding: Hundreds and Thousands

When rounding to the nearest hundred, the key number is in the tens place. If the tens digit is **5** or larger, round up to nearest hundred. If the tens digit is **4** or less, round down to the nearest hundred.

Examples:

Round 871 to the nearest hundred.
7 is the key digit.
If it is more than **5**, round up.
Answer: <u>900</u>

Round 421 to the nearest hundred.
2 is the key digit.
If it is less than **4**, round down.
Answer: <u>400</u>

Directions: Round these numbers to the nearest hundred.

255 _____	368 _____	443 _____	578 _____
562 _____	698 _____	99 _____	775 _____
812 _____	592 _____	124 _____	10,235 _____

When rounding to the nearest thousand, the key number is in the hundreds place. If the hundreds digit is **5** or larger, round up to the nearest thousand. If the hundreds digit is **4** or less, round down to the nearest thousand.

Examples:

Round 7,932 to the nearest thousand.
9 is the key digit.
If it is more than **5**, round up.
Answer: <u>8,000</u>

Round 1,368 to the nearest thousand.
3 is the key digit.
If it is less than **4**, round down.
Answer: <u>1,000</u>

Directions: Round these numbers to the nearest thousand.

8,631 _____	1,248 _____	798 _____
999 _____	6,229 _____	8,461 _____
9,654 _____	4,963 _____	99,923 _____

Rounding

Directions: Round these numbers to the nearest ten.

18 _____ 33 _____ 82 _____ 56 _____

24 _____ 49 _____ 91 _____ 67 _____

Directions: Round these numbers to the nearest hundred.

243 _____ 689 _____ 263 _____ 162 _____

389 _____ 720 _____ 351 _____ 490 _____

463 _____ 846 _____ 928 _____ 733 _____

Directions: Round these numbers to the nearest thousand.

2,638 _____ 3,940 _____ 8,653 _____

6,238 _____ 1,429 _____ 5,061 _____

7,289 _____ 2,742 _____ 9,460 _____

3,109 _____ 4,697 _____ 8,302 _____

Directions: Round these numbers to the nearest ten thousand.

11,368 _____ 38,421 _____

75,302 _____ 67,932 _____

14,569 _____ 49,926 _____

93,694 _____ 81,648 _____

26,784 _____ 87,065 _____

57,843 _____ 29,399 _____

Estimating

To **estimate** means to give an approximate, rather than an exact, answer. To find an estimated sum or difference, round the numbers of the problem, then add or subtract. If the number has **5** ones or more, round up to the nearest ten. If the number has **4** ones or less, round down to the nearest ten.

Directions: Round the numbers to the nearest ten, hundred, or thousand. Then, add or subtract.

Examples:

Ten		Hundred	Thousand
74 → 70 + 39 → + 40 ___ 110	64 → 60 − 25 → − 30 ___ 30	352 → 400 − 164 → − 200 ___ 200	7,681 → 8,000 + 4,321 → + 4,000 ___ 12,000

Round these numbers to the nearest ten.

$$18 \longrightarrow \qquad 49 \longrightarrow \qquad 67 \longrightarrow$$
$$+\,24 \longrightarrow \qquad -\,33 \longrightarrow \qquad -\,56 \longrightarrow$$

Round these numbers to the nearest hundred.

$$255 \longrightarrow \qquad 526 \longrightarrow \qquad 102 \longrightarrow$$
$$-\,99 \longrightarrow \qquad +\,145 \longrightarrow \qquad -\,75 \longrightarrow$$

Round these numbers to the nearest thousand.

$$8{,}361 \longrightarrow \qquad 9{,}926 \longrightarrow$$
$$+\,889 \longrightarrow \qquad +\,3{,}645 \longrightarrow$$

Skip Counting

Skip counting is a quick way to count by skipping numbers. For example, when you skip count by **2**s, you count **2**, **4**, **6**, **8**, and so on. You can skip count by many different numbers such as **2**s, **4**s, **5**s, **10**s, and **100**s.

The illustration below shows skip counting by **2**s to **14**.

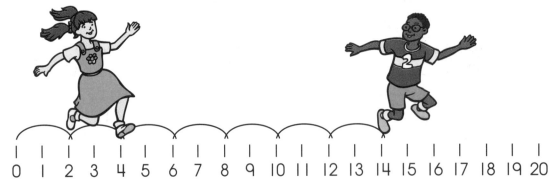

Directions: Use the number line to help you skip count by **2**s from **0** to **20**.

0, _____, _____, _____, 8, _____, _____, 14, _____, _____, _____

Directions: Skip count by **3**s by filling in the rocks across the pond.

Multiplication Facts

5 ···➤ Find the 5 -row.

×6 ···➤ Find the 6 -column.

30 ➤··· The product is named where the 5-row and 6-column meet.

Use the table to multiply.

$$\begin{array}{r} 7 \\ \times 9 \\ \hline \end{array}$$

6-column

5-row ➤

3	0	1	2	3	4	5	6	7	8	9
0	0	0	0	0	0	0	0	0	0	0
1	0	1	2	3	4	5	6	7	8	9
2	0	2	4	6	8	10	12	14	16	18
3	0	3	6	9	12	15	18	21	24	27
4	0	4	8	12	16	20	24	28	32	36
5	0	5	10	15	20	25	(30)	35	40	45
6	0	6	12	18	24	30	36	42	48	54
7	0	7	14	21	28	35	42	49	56	(63)
8	0	8	16	24	32	40	48	56	64	72
9	0	9	18	27	36	45	54	63	72	81

Directions: Multiply.

$\begin{array}{r}6\\\times1\\\hline\end{array}$	$\begin{array}{r}7\\\times8\\\hline\end{array}$	$\begin{array}{r}8\\\times9\\\hline\end{array}$	$\begin{array}{r}9\\\times0\\\hline\end{array}$	$\begin{array}{r}7\\\times7\\\hline\end{array}$	$\begin{array}{r}6\\\times7\\\hline\end{array}$	$\begin{array}{r}7\\\times1\\\hline\end{array}$	$\begin{array}{r}4\\\times6\\\hline\end{array}$
$\begin{array}{r}9\\\times9\\\hline\end{array}$	$\begin{array}{r}6\\\times2\\\hline\end{array}$	$\begin{array}{r}7\\\times6\\\hline\end{array}$	$\begin{array}{r}9\\\times1\\\hline\end{array}$	$\begin{array}{r}8\\\times1\\\hline\end{array}$	$\begin{array}{r}6\\\times8\\\hline\end{array}$	$\begin{array}{r}8\\\times8\\\hline\end{array}$	$\begin{array}{r}3\\\times7\\\hline\end{array}$
$\begin{array}{r}8\\\times0\\\hline\end{array}$	$\begin{array}{r}7\\\times5\\\hline\end{array}$	$\begin{array}{r}6\\\times0\\\hline\end{array}$	$\begin{array}{r}9\\\times2\\\hline\end{array}$	$\begin{array}{r}8\\\times7\\\hline\end{array}$	$\begin{array}{r}6\\\times9\\\hline\end{array}$	$\begin{array}{r}7\\\times0\\\hline\end{array}$	$\begin{array}{r}4\\\times7\\\hline\end{array}$
$\begin{array}{r}5\\\times6\\\hline\end{array}$	$\begin{array}{r}9\\\times3\\\hline\end{array}$	$\begin{array}{r}7\\\times4\\\hline\end{array}$	$\begin{array}{r}6\\\times3\\\hline\end{array}$	$\begin{array}{r}9\\\times4\\\hline\end{array}$	$\begin{array}{r}4\\\times8\\\hline\end{array}$	$\begin{array}{r}8\\\times6\\\hline\end{array}$	$\begin{array}{r}3\\\times6\\\hline\end{array}$
$\begin{array}{r}7\\\times9\\\hline\end{array}$	$\begin{array}{r}5\\\times7\\\hline\end{array}$	$\begin{array}{r}5\\\times8\\\hline\end{array}$	$\begin{array}{r}8\\\times5\\\hline\end{array}$	$\begin{array}{r}6\\\times4\\\hline\end{array}$	$\begin{array}{r}7\\\times3\\\hline\end{array}$	$\begin{array}{r}9\\\times5\\\hline\end{array}$	$\begin{array}{r}2\\\times6\\\hline\end{array}$
$\begin{array}{r}7\\\times2\\\hline\end{array}$	$\begin{array}{r}8\\\times4\\\hline\end{array}$	$\begin{array}{r}9\\\times6\\\hline\end{array}$	$\begin{array}{r}9\\\times7\\\hline\end{array}$	$\begin{array}{r}4\\\times9\\\hline\end{array}$	$\begin{array}{r}6\\\times5\\\hline\end{array}$	$\begin{array}{r}9\\\times8\\\hline\end{array}$	$\begin{array}{r}2\\\times8\\\hline\end{array}$
$\begin{array}{r}8\\\times3\\\hline\end{array}$	$\begin{array}{r}5\\\times9\\\hline\end{array}$	$\begin{array}{r}3\\\times8\\\hline\end{array}$	$\begin{array}{r}8\\\times2\\\hline\end{array}$	$\begin{array}{r}3\\\times9\\\hline\end{array}$	$\begin{array}{r}2\\\times7\\\hline\end{array}$	$\begin{array}{r}6\\\times6\\\hline\end{array}$	$\begin{array}{r}2\\\times9\\\hline\end{array}$

Math: Grade 4

Fact Factory

Factors are the numbers multiplied together in a multiplication problem. The **product** is the answer.

Directions: Write the missing factors or products.

X	5
1	5
5	
4	20
6	
3	
2	10
7	
9	45

X	9
8	72
3	
4	
9	
6	54
7	
2	
1	9

X	7
2	14
5	
	42
8	
7	
4	
	21
0	

X	3
7	
4	
6	
1	
3	
2	
5	
8	

X	1
1	
12	
10	
3	3
5	
7	
6	
4	

X	8
9	
8	
4	
5	
6	
7	
3	
2	

X	2
24	
2	
22	
4	
20	
6	
18	
8	

X	4
2	
4	
6	
8	
	4
	12
	20
	28

X	6
7	
6	
5	
4	
3	
2	
1	
0	

X	10
	20
3	
	40
5	
	60
7	
	80
9	

X	11
4	
7	
9	
10	
3	
5	
6	
8	

X	12
1	
2	24
3	
4	48
5	
6	
7	
8	

Multiplication

$$\begin{array}{r} 4 \\ \times 2 \\ \hline 8 \end{array} \qquad \begin{array}{r} 40 \\ \times 2 \\ \hline 80 \end{array}$$

If $2 \times 4 = 8$,
then $2 \times 40 = 80$.

Multiply 3 ones by 2.   Multiply 4 tens by 2.

$$\begin{array}{r} 43 \\ \times 2 \\ \hline \end{array} \qquad \begin{array}{r} 43 \\ \times 2 \\ \hline 6 \end{array} \qquad \begin{array}{r} 43 \\ \times 2 \\ \hline 86 \end{array}$$

Directions: Multiply.

$\begin{array}{r}3\\\times 3\\\hline\end{array}$	$\begin{array}{r}30\\\times 3\\\hline\end{array}$	$\begin{array}{r}2\\\times 4\\\hline\end{array}$	$\begin{array}{r}20\\\times 4\\\hline\end{array}$	$\begin{array}{r}3\\\times 2\\\hline\end{array}$	$\begin{array}{r}30\\\times 2\\\hline\end{array}$
$\begin{array}{r}2\\\times 3\\\hline\end{array}$	$\begin{array}{r}30\\\times 3\\\hline\end{array}$	$\begin{array}{r}32\\\times 3\\\hline\end{array}$	$\begin{array}{r}1\\\times 2\\\hline\end{array}$	$\begin{array}{r}40\\\times 2\\\hline\end{array}$	$\begin{array}{r}41\\\times 2\\\hline\end{array}$
$\begin{array}{r}11\\\times 9\\\hline\end{array}$	$\begin{array}{r}33\\\times 3\\\hline\end{array}$	$\begin{array}{r}12\\\times 3\\\hline\end{array}$	$\begin{array}{r}14\\\times 2\\\hline\end{array}$	$\begin{array}{r}31\\\times 3\\\hline\end{array}$	$\begin{array}{r}13\\\times 3\\\hline\end{array}$
$\begin{array}{r}32\\\times 2\\\hline\end{array}$	$\begin{array}{r}23\\\times 3\\\hline\end{array}$	$\begin{array}{r}42\\\times 2\\\hline\end{array}$	$\begin{array}{r}21\\\times 4\\\hline\end{array}$	$\begin{array}{r}13\\\times 2\\\hline\end{array}$	$\begin{array}{r}11\\\times 6\\\hline\end{array}$
$\begin{array}{r}12\\\times 2\\\hline\end{array}$	$\begin{array}{r}11\\\times 5\\\hline\end{array}$	$\begin{array}{r}33\\\times 2\\\hline\end{array}$	$\begin{array}{r}11\\\times 3\\\hline\end{array}$	$\begin{array}{r}21\\\times 2\\\hline\end{array}$	$\begin{array}{r}22\\\times 3\\\hline\end{array}$
$\begin{array}{r}11\\\times 4\\\hline\end{array}$	$\begin{array}{r}44\\\times 2\\\hline\end{array}$	$\begin{array}{r}22\\\times 2\\\hline\end{array}$	$\begin{array}{r}11\\\times 8\\\hline\end{array}$	$\begin{array}{r}11\\\times 2\\\hline\end{array}$	$\begin{array}{r}13\\\times 2\\\hline\end{array}$
$\begin{array}{r}23\\\times 2\\\hline\end{array}$	$\begin{array}{r}22\\\times 4\\\hline\end{array}$	$\begin{array}{r}24\\\times 2\\\hline\end{array}$	$\begin{array}{r}21\\\times 3\\\hline\end{array}$	$\begin{array}{r}31\\\times 2\\\hline\end{array}$	$\begin{array}{r}11\\\times 7\\\hline\end{array}$

Multiplying and Regrouping

1. Multiply 3 x 8 in the ones column. Ask: Do I need to regroup?

2. Multiply 3 x 3 in the tens column. Add the 2 you carried over from the ones column. Ask: Do I need to regroup?

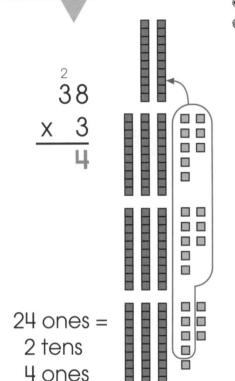

²
38
x 3
___
   4

24 ones =
2 tens
4 ones

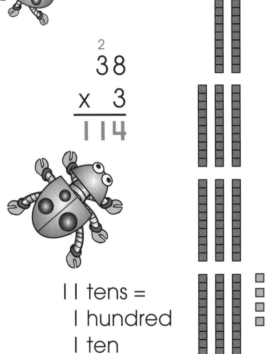

²
38
x 3
___
114

11 tens =
1 hundred
1 ten

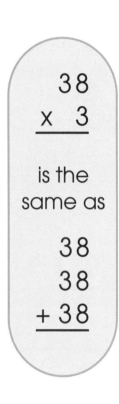

38
x 3
___

is the
same as

38
38
+ 38
_____

Directions: Multiply.

| 29 | 62 | 39 | 86 | 43 |
| x 3 | x 4 | x 4 | x 7 | x 6 |

| 28 | 48 | 31 | 25 | 55 |
| x 6 | x 2 | x 9 | x 5 | x 5 |

Hmm, What Should I Do?

Examples: 52 $(+)$ 9 = 61   37 $(-)$ 8 = 29

8 (X) 4 = 32   28 $(\div)$ 7 = 4

Directions: Write the correct symbols in the circles.

7 $\bigcirc$ 8 = 56   81 $\bigcirc$ 6 = 75   55 $\bigcirc$ 3 = 52

54 $\bigcirc$ 9 = 6   2 $\bigcirc$ 1 = 2   40 $\bigcirc$ 2 = 38

36 $\bigcirc$ 5 = 31   0 $\bigcirc$ 2 = 2   8 $\bigcirc$ 8 = 64

12 $\bigcirc$ 6 = 18   9 $\bigcirc$ 8 = 72   18 $\bigcirc$ 5 = 23

72 $\bigcirc$ 7 = 65   32 $\bigcirc$ 5 = 37

0 $\bigcirc$ 1 = 0      48 $\bigcirc$ 6 = 8

9 $\bigcirc$ 1 = 9   32 $\bigcirc$ 4 = 8

45 $\bigcirc$ 9 = 5   6 $\bigcirc$ 7 = 42

Multiplication: Tens, Hundreds, Thousands

When multiplying a number by **10**, the answer is the number with a **0**. It is like counting by tens.

Examples:

```
  10      10      10      10      10      10
x  1    x  2    x  3    x  4    x  5    x  6
----    ----    ----    ----    ----    ----
  10      20      30      40      50      60
```

When multiplying a number by **100**, the answer is a number with two **0**s. When multiplying by **1,000**, the answer is a number with three **0**s.

Examples:

```
  100        100        100      1,000      1,000      1,000
x   1      x   2      x   3      x   1      x   2      x   3
-----      -----      -----      ------     ------     ------
  100        200        300      1,000      2,000      3,000


    4        400          8        800          7        700
x   2      x   2      x   3      x   3      x   5      x   5
-----      -----      -----      ------     -----      ------
    8        800         24      2,400         35      3,500
```

Directions: Multiply.

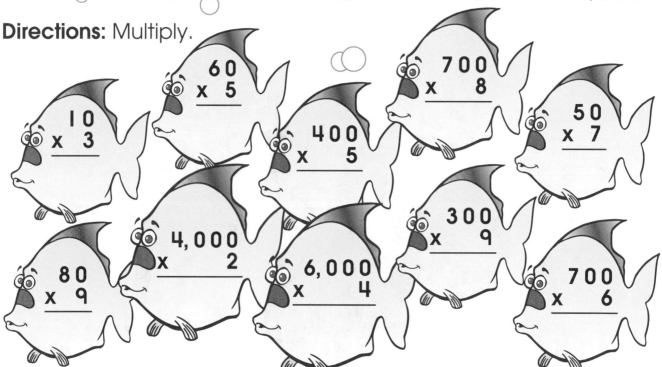

Name _____

Multiplication: Two-Digit Numbers Times Two-Digit Numbers

Follow the steps for multiplying a two-digit number by a two-digit number using regrouping.

Example:

Step 1: Multiply the ones. Regroup.

```
            2
   63      63
 x 68    x 68
         ────
          504
```

Step 2: Multiply the tens. Regroup. Add.

```
           1
   63        63
 x 68      x 68
 ────      ────
 3,780      504
         +3,780
         ──────
          4,284
```

Directions: Multiply.

```
   12      27      65      19      99      35
 x 55    x 15    x 27    x 39    x 13    x 14
```

```
   43      38      53      47      57      48
 x 26    x 17    x 86    x 72    x 62    x 33
```

```
   27      93      64      53
 x 54    x 45    x 16    x 23
```

The Jones farm has 24 cows that each produce 52 quarts of milk a day. How many quarts are produced each day altogether? _____

Multiplication: Three-Digit Numbers
Times Three-Digit Numbers

Directions: Multiply. Regroup when needed.

Example:
```
      5 6 3
    x 2 4 8
    ─────────
      4, 5 0 4
     2 2, 5 2 0
   + 1 1 2, 6 0 0
    ─────────
   1 3 9, 6 2 4
```

Hint: When multiplying by the tens, start writing the number in the tens place. When multiplying by the hundreds, start in the hundreds place.

```
  8 4 2        9 3 2        7 5 9        5 3 1
x 1 6 7      x 2 7 2      x 4 6 8      x 5 5 6
```

```
  3 8 3        5 2 3        2 2 9        7 3 8
x 4 7 6      x 3 4 9      x 1 8 9      x 5 1 3
```

James grows pumpkins on his farm. He has 362 rows of pumpkins. There are 593 pumpkins in each row.

How many pumpkins does James grow? _____

24

Division

Division is a way to find out how many times one number is contained in another number. For example, $28 \div 7 = 4$ means that there are 4 groups of 7 in 28.

Division problems can be written two ways: $36 \div 6 = 6$ or $6\overline{)36}$ with quotient 6.

These are the parts of a division problem:

dividend $\longrightarrow 36 \div 6 = 6 \longleftarrow$ quotient
divisor

divisor $\longrightarrow 6\overline{)36}$ — $6 \longleftarrow$ quotient, $36 \longleftarrow$ dividend

Directions: Divide.

$7\overline{)21}$ $2\overline{)2}$ $5\overline{)25}$

$9\overline{)45}$ $4\overline{)32}$

$2\overline{)4}$

$4\overline{)12}$ $8\overline{)24}$ $6\overline{)24}$ $3\overline{)6}$

$7\overline{)14}$ $9\overline{)54}$ $5\overline{)15}$ $3\overline{)9}$

$6\overline{)12}$ $64 \div 8 =$ _____ $63 \div 7 =$ _____

$81 \div 9 =$ _____

$72 \div 8 =$ _____

$6\overline{)36}$ $7\overline{)49}$

$6\overline{)48}$ $5\overline{)40}$ $27 \div 3 =$ _____ $16 \div 4 =$ _____

$72 \div 9 =$ _____

Division Facts

$\overset{4}{3)\,12}$ → Find the 12 in the 3 -column.

The quotient is named in the ▨ at the end of this row.

Use the table to divide.

$5)\,30$

×	0	1	2	3	4	5	6	7	8	9
0	0	0	0	0	0	0	0	0	0	0
1	0	1	2	3	4	5	6	7	8	9
2	0	2	4	6	8	10	12	14	16	18
3	0	3	6	9	12	15	18	21	24	27
4	0	4	8	12	16	20	24	28	32	36
5	0	5	10	15	20	25	30	35	40	45
6	0	6	12	18	24	30	36	42	48	54
7	0	7	14	21	28	35	42	49	56	63
8	0	8	16	24	32	40	48	56	64	72
9	0	9	18	27	36	45	54	63	72	81

Directions: Divide.

$3)\,15$	$4)\,12$	$1)\,7$	$5)\,25$	$2)\,12$	$4)\,28$
$5)\,35$	$2)\,14$	$3)\,18$	$4)\,20$	$1)\,9$	$3)\,9$
$4)\,32$	$5)\,20$	$1)\,6$	$3)\,12$	$2)\,10$	$3)\,21$
$2)\,16$	$3)\,3$	$4)\,16$	$1)\,8$	$4)\,0$	$5)\,10$
$3)\,24$	$5)\,0$	$2)\,8$	$4)\,36$	$5)\,15$	$3)\,27$
$4)\,24$	$2)\,18$	$5)\,40$	$3)\,0$	$1)\,5$	$5)\,45$
$1)\,4$	$2)\,6$	$5)\,30$	$5)\,5$	$4)\,8$	$3)\,6$

Name _____

Two-Digit Quotients

Directions: Follow the steps below. Then divide.

1. Ask: Is the tens digit large enough to divide into? (Yes.) Divide. Multiply the partial quotient (2) by the divisor (4) and subtract from the partial dividend (8).

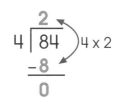

$3\overline{)63}$ $2\overline{)72}$

8 tens divided into 4 groups. How many are in each group? (2)

$4\overline{)48}$ $2\overline{)56}$

2. Carry down the 4 in the ones column. Ask: How many groups of 4 are there in 4? (1) Divide. Multiply the partial quotient (1) by the divisor (4) and subtract from the partial dividend (4).

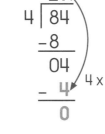

$3\overline{)96}$ $2\overline{)82}$

3. When 84 things are divided into 4 groups, there will be 21 in each group.

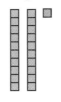 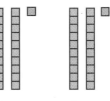 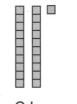 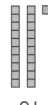

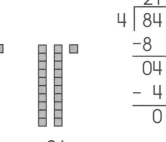

$84 \div 4 = 21 + 21 + 21 + 21$

Division Facts

$$\begin{array}{r} 5 \\ \times\,6 \\ \hline 30 \end{array} \longrightarrow 6\,\overline{)\,30}^{\,5}$$

$$\begin{array}{r} 5 \\ \times\,7 \\ \hline 35 \end{array} \longrightarrow 7\,\overline{)\,35}^{\,5}$$

$6 \times 5 = 30$, so $30 \div 6 = \underline{\ \ 5\ \ }$.

$7 \times 5 = 35$, so $35 \div 7 = \underline{\ \ 5\ \ }$.

Directions: Complete the following.

$$\begin{array}{r} 6 \\ \times\,6 \\ \hline 36 \end{array} \text{ so } 6\,\overline{)\,36}$$
$$\begin{array}{r} 7 \\ \times\,6 \\ \hline 42 \end{array} \text{ so } 6\,\overline{)\,42}$$
$$\begin{array}{r} 8 \\ \times\,6 \\ \hline 48 \end{array} \text{ so } 6\,\overline{)\,48}$$
$$\begin{array}{r} 9 \\ \times\,6 \\ \hline 54 \end{array} \text{ so } 6\,\overline{)\,54}$$

$$\begin{array}{r} 6 \\ \times\,7 \\ \hline 42 \end{array} \text{ so } 7\,\overline{)\,42}$$
$$\begin{array}{r} 7 \\ \times\,7 \\ \hline 49 \end{array} \text{ so } 7\,\overline{)\,49}$$
$$\begin{array}{r} 8 \\ \times\,7 \\ \hline 56 \end{array} \text{ so } 7\,\overline{)\,56}$$
$$\begin{array}{r} 9 \\ \times\,7 \\ \hline 63 \end{array} \text{ so } 7\,\overline{)\,63}$$

Directions: Divide.

$6\,\overline{)\,54}$ $7\,\overline{)\,14}$ $6\,\overline{)\,30}$ $7\,\overline{)\,35}$ $6\,\overline{)\,6}$

$7\,\overline{)\,49}$ $6\,\overline{)\,42}$ $7\,\overline{)\,42}$ $6\,\overline{)\,0}$ $7\,\overline{)\,21}$

$6\,\overline{)\,18}$ $7\,\overline{)\,7}$ $6\,\overline{)\,36}$ $7\,\overline{)\,56}$ $6\,\overline{)\,24}$

$7\,\overline{)\,28}$ $6\,\overline{)\,48}$ $7\,\overline{)\,0}$ $6\,\overline{)\,12}$ $7\,\overline{)\,63}$

$4\,\overline{)\,16}$ $4\,\overline{)\,28}$ $5\,\overline{)\,20}$ $5\,\overline{)\,35}$ $4\,\overline{)\,36}$

Division: Checking the Answers

Directions: To check a division problem, multiply the quotient by the divisor. Add the remainder. The answer will be the dividend.

Example:

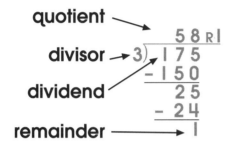

```
       quotient
                    58 R1
       divisor → 3) 1 7 5
                  - 1 5 0
       dividend     2 5
                  -  2 4
       remainder →   1
```

```
   58 ← quotient
  x  3 ← divisor
  174
+    1 ← remainder
  175 ← dividend
```

Directions: Divide each problem, then draw a line from the division problem to the correct checking problem.

```
   33        53        97       135       113       119
  x 7       x 7       x 7       x 7       x 7       x 7
           + 2       + 3       + 1       + 1       + 1
```

```
7)682    7)231    7)373    7)792    7)834    7)946
```

The toy factory puts 7 robot dogs in each box. The factory has 256 robot dogs. How many boxes will they need?

_____

Division: Larger Numbers

Follow the steps for dividing larger numbers.

Example: **Step 1:** Divide the tens first. **Step 2:** Divide the ones next.

```
                    2                        2 2
3)66          3)6 6                    3)6 6
             -6                        -6
              0 6                       0 6
                                      - 6
                                        0
```

Directions: Divide.

4)8 4   2)9 0   2)6 4   2)5 0   3)4 5

3)7 5   3)3 6   4)9 2   2)7 6   5)65

In some larger numbers, the divisor goes into the first two digits of the dividend.

Example:
```
              8                    8 1
9)7 2 9    9)7 2 9          9)7 2 9
           -7 2              -7 2
             0 9              0 9
                           -  9
                              0
```

Directions: Divide.

7)6 3 0   5)1 2 5   6)4 8 6   5)1 0 0   6)5 4 0

Name _____

Division: Two-Digit Divisors

Directions: Divide. Then check each answer on another sheet of paper by multiplying it by the divisor and adding the remainder.

Example:

```
      2              2 1 R4
12)256         12)256
  -24             -24
    1              16
                  -12
                    4
```

Check:

```
    2 1
  x 1 2
  ─────
    4 2
  2 1 0
  ─────
  2 5 2
  +   4
  ─────
  2 5 6
```

```
27)880      81)913      65)790      42)674      67)823
```

```
72)977      54)743      45)863      24)432      18)372
```

```
28)175      49)538      77)936      37)603      63)835
```

The Allen farm has 882 chickens. The chickens are kept in 21 coops. How many chickens are there in each coop?

_____

Averaging

An **average** is found by adding two or more quantities and dividing by the number of quantities.

Example:

Step 1: Find the sum of the numbers.
24 + 36 + 30 = **90**

Step 2: Divide by the number of quantities.
90 ÷ 3 = **30**

The average is 30.

Directions: Find the average of each group of numbers. Draw a line from each problem to the correct average.

12 + 14 + 29 + 1 =	410
4 + 10 + 25 =	83
33 + 17 + 14 + 20 + 16 =	40
782 + 276 + 172 =	15
81 + 82 + 91 + 78 =	13
21 + 34 + 44 =	33
14 + 24 + 10 + 31 + 5 + 6 =	14
278 + 246 =	20
48 + 32 + 18 + 62 =	262

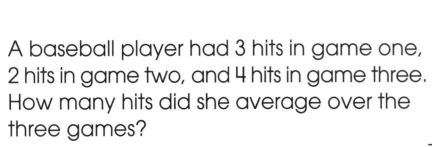

A baseball player had 3 hits in game one, 2 hits in game two, and 4 hits in game three. How many hits did she average over the three games?

_____

Geometry: Polygons

A **polygon** is a closed figure with three or more sides.

Examples:

triangle	**square**	**rectangle**	**pentagon**	**hexagon**	**octagon**
3 sides	4 equal sides	4 sides	5 sides	6 sides	8 sides

Directions: Identify the polygons.

 _____

 _____

 _____

 _____

 _____

 _____

Math: Grade 4

Geometry: Angles

The point at which two line segments meet is called an **angle**. There are three types of angles — right, acute, and obtuse.

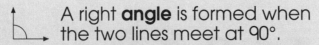

A right **angle** is formed when the two lines meet at 90°.

An **acute angle** is formed when the two lines meet at less than 90°.

An **obtuse angle** is formed when the two lines meet at greater than 90°.

Angles can be measured with a protractor or index card. With a protractor, align the bottom edge of the angle with the bottom of the protractor, with the angle point at the circle of the protractor. Note the direction of the other ray and the number of degrees of the angle.

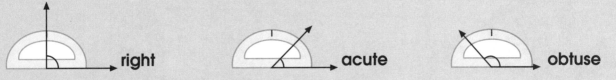

Place the corner of an index card in the corner of the angle. If the edges line up with the card, it is a right angle. If not, the angle is acute or obtuse.

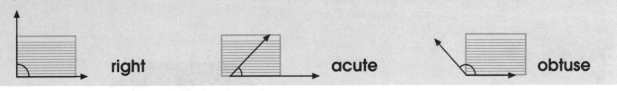

Directions: Use a protractor or index card to identify the following angles as right, obtuse, or acute.

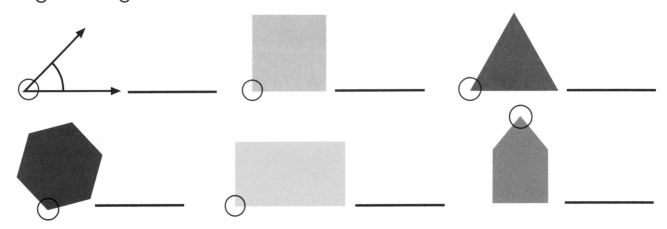

Fractions

Directions: Name the fraction that is shaded.

Examples:

3 of 4 equal parts are shaded.

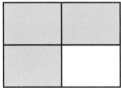

$$\frac{3}{4}$$

12 of 16 equal parts are shaded.

$$\frac{12}{16}$$

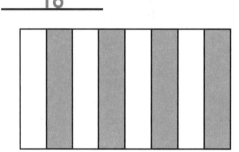

_____   _____   _____

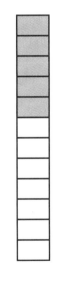

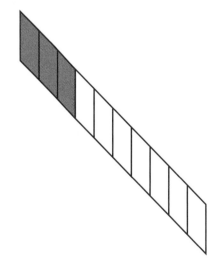

_____   _____   _____

Working With Fractions

Directions: Use the fraction bars to help you find the smallest fraction in each row. Circle it.

1. $\dfrac{1}{2}$ $\dfrac{2}{3}$ $\dfrac{1}{6}$ $\dfrac{1}{3}$

2. $\dfrac{2}{3}$ $\dfrac{2}{6}$ $\dfrac{3}{3}$ $\dfrac{3}{6}$

3. $\dfrac{2}{2}$ $\dfrac{3}{6}$ $\dfrac{2}{3}$ $\dfrac{1}{3}$

4. $\dfrac{5}{6}$ $\dfrac{4}{6}$ $\dfrac{1}{2}$ $\dfrac{2}{3}$

5. $\dfrac{6}{6}$ $\dfrac{2}{3}$ $\dfrac{5}{6}$ $\dfrac{2}{2}$

1 Whole					
$\frac{1}{2}$			$\frac{2}{2}$		
$\frac{1}{3}$		$\frac{2}{3}$		$\frac{3}{3}$	
$\frac{1}{6}$	$\frac{2}{6}$	$\frac{3}{6}$	$\frac{4}{6}$	$\frac{5}{6}$	$\frac{6}{6}$

Directions: Use the fraction bars to help you find the greatest fraction in each row. Circle it.

1 Whole							
$\frac{1}{2}$				$\frac{2}{2}$			
$\frac{1}{4}$		$\frac{2}{4}$		$\frac{3}{4}$		$\frac{4}{4}$	
$\frac{1}{8}$	$\frac{2}{8}$	$\frac{3}{8}$	$\frac{4}{8}$	$\frac{5}{8}$	$\frac{6}{8}$	$\frac{7}{8}$	$\frac{8}{8}$

1. $\dfrac{1}{2}$ $\dfrac{3}{4}$ $\dfrac{6}{8}$ $\dfrac{8}{8}$

2. $\dfrac{1}{4}$ $\dfrac{1}{8}$ $\dfrac{7}{8}$ $\dfrac{1}{2}$

3. $\dfrac{1}{8}$ $\dfrac{1}{2}$ $\dfrac{1}{4}$ $\dfrac{2}{8}$

4. $\dfrac{1}{4}$ $\dfrac{3}{8}$ $\dfrac{5}{8}$ $\dfrac{3}{4}$

5. $\dfrac{2}{8}$ $\dfrac{1}{8}$ $\dfrac{1}{4}$ $\dfrac{6}{8}$

Name _____

Equivalent Fractions

Equivalent fractions are two different fractions that represent the same number. **Example:**  $\frac{1}{2}$ = $\frac{3}{6}$

Directions: Complete these equivalent fractions.

$\frac{1}{3} = \frac{}{6}$ $\qquad$ $\frac{1}{2} = \frac{}{4}$ $\qquad$ $\frac{3}{4} = \frac{}{8}$ $\qquad$ $\frac{1}{3} = \frac{}{9}$

Directions: Circle the figures that show a fraction equivalent to figure A. Write the fraction for the shaded area under each figure.

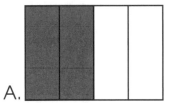   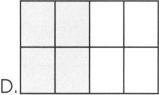

A. _____ B. _____ C. _____ D. _____

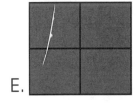 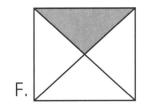 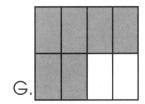 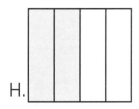

E. _____ F. _____ G. _____ H. _____

To find an equivalent fraction, multiply both parts of the fraction by the same number.

Example: $\frac{2}{3} \times \frac{3}{3} = \frac{6}{9}$

Directions: Find an equivalent fraction.

$\frac{1}{4} = \frac{}{8}$ $\qquad$ $\frac{3}{4} = \frac{}{16}$ $\qquad$ $\frac{4}{5} = \frac{8}{}$ $\qquad$ $\frac{3}{8} = \frac{}{24}$

Fractions: Addition

When adding fractions with the same denominator, the denominator stays the same. Add only the numerators.

Example: numerator
denominator $\dfrac{1}{8} + \dfrac{2}{8} = \dfrac{3}{8}$

Directions: Add the fractions on the flowers. Begin in the center of each flower and add each petal. The first one is done for you.

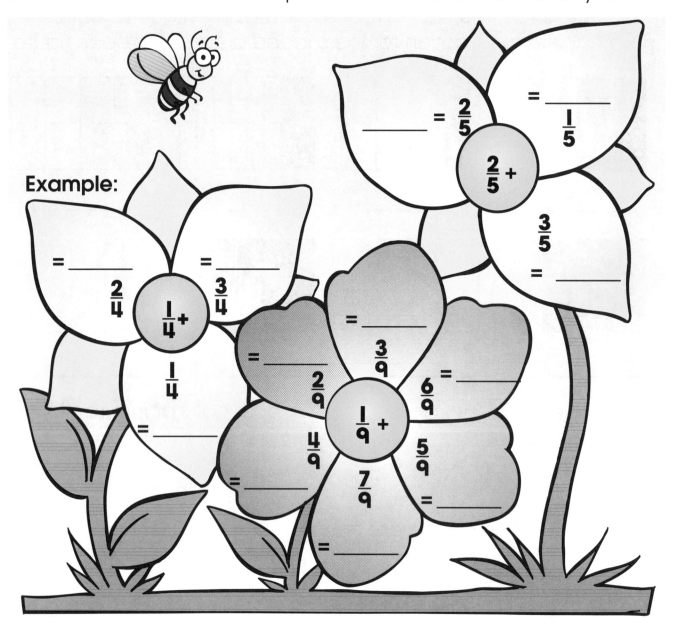

Name _____

Fractions: Subtraction

When subtracting fractions with the same denominator, the denominator stays the same. Subtract only the numerators.

Directions: Solve the problems, working from left to right. As you find each answer, copy the letter from the key into the numbered blanks. The answer is the name of a famous American. The first one is done for you.

1. $\dfrac{3}{8} - \dfrac{2}{8} = \dfrac{1}{8}$

2. $\dfrac{2}{4} - \dfrac{1}{4} =$ ____

3. $\dfrac{5}{9} - \dfrac{3}{9} =$ ____

4. $\dfrac{2}{3} - \dfrac{1}{3} =$ ____

5. $\dfrac{8}{12} - \dfrac{7}{12} =$ ____

6. $\dfrac{4}{5} - \dfrac{1}{5} =$ ____

7. $\dfrac{6}{12} - \dfrac{3}{12} =$ ____

8. $\dfrac{4}{9} - \dfrac{1}{9} =$ ____

9. $\dfrac{11}{12} - \dfrac{7}{12} =$ ____

10. $\dfrac{7}{8} - \dfrac{3}{8} =$ ____

11. $\dfrac{4}{7} - \dfrac{2}{7} =$ ____

12. $\dfrac{14}{16} - \dfrac{7}{16} =$ ____

13. $\dfrac{18}{20} - \dfrac{13}{20} =$ ____

14. $\dfrac{13}{15} - \dfrac{2}{15} =$ ____

15. $\dfrac{5}{6} - \dfrac{3}{6} =$ ____

T $\dfrac{1}{8}$	P $\dfrac{5}{24}$	H $\dfrac{1}{4}$
F $\dfrac{4}{12}$	E $\dfrac{2}{7}$	J $\dfrac{3}{12}$
E $\dfrac{3}{9}$	O $\dfrac{2}{9}$	F $\dfrac{4}{8}$
R $\dfrac{7}{16}$	O $\dfrac{2}{8}$	Y $\dfrac{8}{20}$
Q $\dfrac{1}{32}$	M $\dfrac{1}{3}$	S $\dfrac{5}{20}$
A $\dfrac{1}{12}$	R $\dfrac{12}{15}$	S $\dfrac{3}{5}$
N $\dfrac{2}{6}$	O $\dfrac{11}{15}$	

Who helped write the Declaration of Independence?

$\dfrac{T}{1}$ $\dfrac{}{2}$ $\dfrac{}{3}$ $\dfrac{}{4}$ $\dfrac{}{5}$ $\dfrac{}{6}$ $\dfrac{}{7}$ $\dfrac{}{8}$ $\dfrac{}{9}$ $\dfrac{}{10}$ $\dfrac{}{11}$ $\dfrac{}{12}$ $\dfrac{}{13}$ $\dfrac{}{14}$ $\dfrac{}{15}$

 Math: Grade 4

Name _____

Reducing Fractions

Reducing a fraction means to find the greatest common factor and divide.

Example: $\dfrac{5}{15}$ factors of 5: 1, 5
factors of 15: 1, 3, 5, 15

5 is the greatest common factor. Divide both the numerator and denominator by **5**.

$5 \div 5 = 1$
$15 \div 5 = 3$

Directions: Reduce each fraction. Circle the correct answer.

$\dfrac{2}{4} = \dfrac{1}{2}, \dfrac{1}{6}, \dfrac{1}{8}$ $\dfrac{3}{9} = \dfrac{1}{6}, \dfrac{1}{3}, \dfrac{3}{6}$ $\dfrac{5}{10} = \dfrac{1}{5}, \dfrac{1}{2}, \dfrac{5}{6}$ $\dfrac{4}{12} = \dfrac{1}{4}, \dfrac{1}{3}, \dfrac{2}{3}$ $\dfrac{10}{15} = \dfrac{2}{3}, \dfrac{2}{5}, \dfrac{2}{7}$

$\dfrac{12}{14} = \dfrac{1}{8}, \dfrac{6}{7}, \dfrac{3}{5}$ $\dfrac{3}{24} = \dfrac{2}{12}, \dfrac{3}{6}, \dfrac{1}{8}$ $\dfrac{1}{11} = \dfrac{1}{11}, \dfrac{2}{5}, \dfrac{3}{4}$ $\dfrac{11}{22} = \dfrac{1}{12}, \dfrac{1}{2}, \dfrac{2}{5}$

Directions: Find the way home. Color the boxes with fractions equivalent to $\frac{1}{8}$ and $\frac{1}{3}$.

		$\dfrac{4}{5}$			$\dfrac{6}{48}$	$\dfrac{3}{24}$	
$\dfrac{4}{9}$	$\dfrac{2}{6}$	$\dfrac{5}{6}$					$\dfrac{3}{5}$
		$\dfrac{2}{16}$	$\dfrac{7}{32}$	$\dfrac{10}{33}$	$\dfrac{2}{8}$	$\dfrac{5}{15}$	
$\dfrac{5}{12}$		$\dfrac{5}{8}$	$\dfrac{9}{27}$		$\dfrac{1}{4}$	$\dfrac{2}{12}$	$\dfrac{1}{2}$
		$\dfrac{4}{16}$		$\dfrac{6}{18}$		$\dfrac{8}{24}$	$\dfrac{4}{32}$
$\dfrac{3}{7}$		$\dfrac{2}{21}$		$\dfrac{3}{5}$			

Fractions: Adding Mixed Numbers

When adding mixed numbers, add the fractions first, then the whole numbers.

Examples:

$$9\frac{1}{3}$$
$$+3\frac{1}{3}$$
$$\overline{12\frac{2}{3}}$$

$$2\frac{3}{6}$$
$$+1\frac{1}{6}$$
$$\overline{3\frac{4}{6}}$$

Directions: Add the number in the center to the number in each surrounding section.

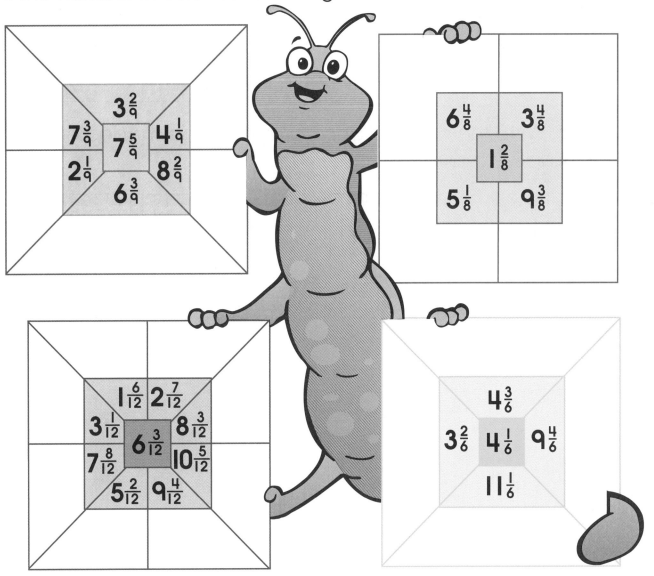

Fractions to Decimals

When a figure is divided into 10 equal parts, the parts are called **tenths.** Tenths can be written two ways—as a fraction or a decimal. A **decimal** is a number with one or more places to the right of a decimal point, such as 6.5 or 2.25. A **decimal point** is the dot between the ones place and the tenths place.

Examples:

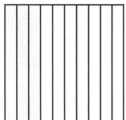

ones	tenths
0 .	3

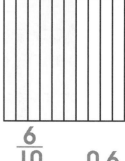

$\frac{3}{10}$ or 0.3 of the square is shaded.

$\frac{6}{10}$ 0.6

Directions: Write the decimal and fraction for the shaded parts of the following figures.

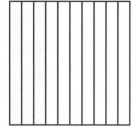

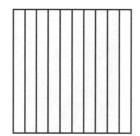

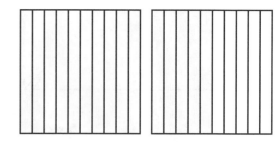

_____   _____   _____   _____   _____   _____

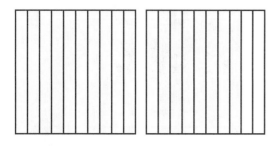

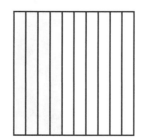

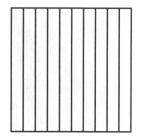

_____   _____   _____   _____   _____   _____

Name _____

Decimals

Directions: Add or subtract. Remember to include the decimal point in your answers.

Example:

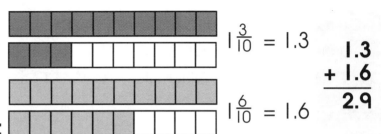

$1\frac{3}{10} = 1.3$

$1\frac{6}{10} = 1.6$

```
  1.3
+ 1.6
─────
  2.9
```

8.1 + 1.7	4.1 + 6.2	0.5 + 1.6	7.6 − 6.5	7.2 − 2.6	1.2 + 5.0	8.7 − 3.9	6.8 − 3.7

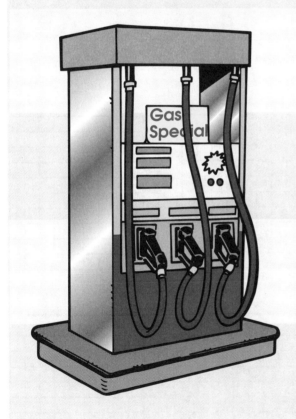

7.8 − 6.8	16.5 − 7.3	6.4 + 5.3	10.0 + 3.5
0.42 + 0.35	0.98 − 0.87	0.78 − 0.13	0.83 + 0.12
0.95 − 0.14	3.23 + 2.48	4.68 − 2.65	5.86 − 2.73
6.98 + 1.40	3.27 + 1.82	4.65 − 1.32	5.97 + 2.77

Mr. Martin went on a car trip with his family. Mr. Martin purchased gas 3 times. He bought 6.7 gallons, 7.3 gallons, then 5.8 gallons of gas. How much gas did he purchase in all?

_____

Decimals: Hundredths

The next smallest decimal unit after a tenth is called a **hundredth**. One hundredth is one unit of a figure divided into 100 units. Written as a decimal, it is one digit to the right of the tenths place.

Example:

One square divided into hundredths, 34 hundredths are shaded. Write: 0.34.

ones	tenths	hundredths
0 .	3	4

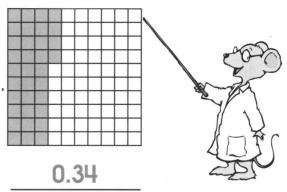

0.34

Directions: Write the decimal for the shaded parts of the following figures.

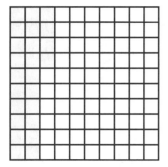 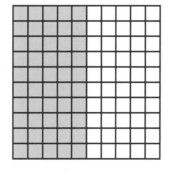 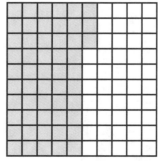 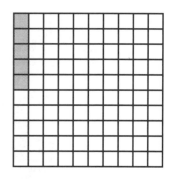

_____   _____   _____   _____

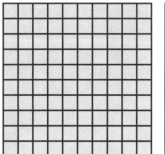  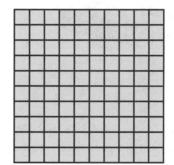 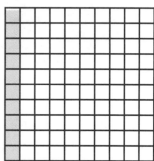

_____   _____

Graphing

A **graph** is a drawing that shows information about changes in numbers.

Directions: Answer the questions by reading the graphs.

Bar Graph

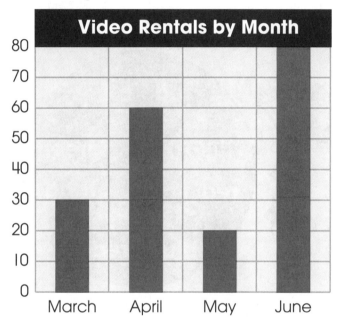

How many videos did the store rent in June?

_____

In which month did the store rent the fewest videos?

_____

How many videos did the store rent for all 4 months?

_____

Line Graph

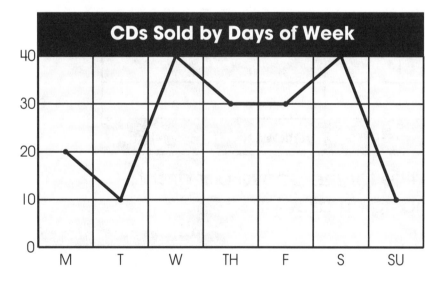

On which days did the store sell the fewest CDs?

_____

How many CDs did the store sell in 1 week?

_____

Guess the Color

Probability shows the chance that a given event will happen. To show probability, write a fraction. The number of different possibilities is the denominator. The number of times the event could happen is the numerator. (Remember to reduce fractions to the lowest terms.)

Directions: Look at the spinner. What is the probability that the arrow will land on . . .

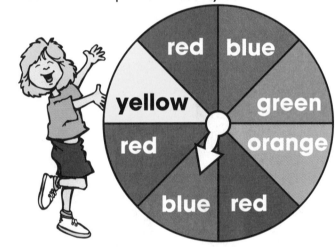

1. red? $\frac{3}{8}$

2. blue?   _____

3. yellow? _____

4. green? _____

5. orange?_____

Directions: Complete the bar graph showing your answers (the data) from above.

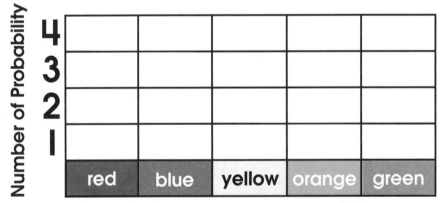

Directions: Circle the best title for the above bar graph.
a. Probability of Arrow Landing on a Color
b. Eight Turns of the Spinner
c. Which Color Is the Winner?

Name _____

Graphing: Finding Ordered Pairs

Graphs or grids are sometimes used to find the location of objects.

Example: The ice-cream cone is located at point (5, 6) on the graph. To find the ice cream's location, follow the line to the bottom of the grid to get the first number — 5. Then go back to the ice cream and follow the grid line to the left for the second number — 6.

Directions: Write the ordered pair for the following objects. The first one is done for you.

book __(4, 8)__   bike_____   suitcase _____   house   _____

globe_____   cup _____   triangle _____   airplane _____

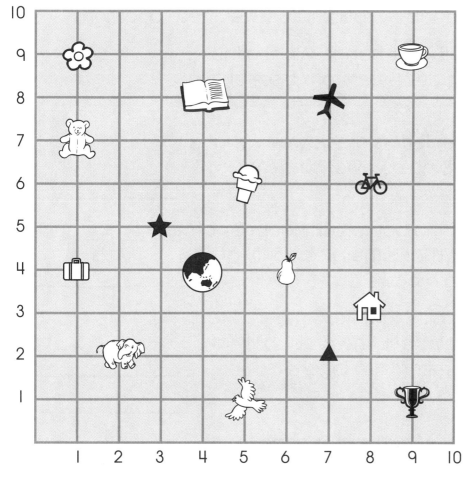

Directions: Identify the objects located at the following points. The first one is done for you.

(9, 1) ____trophy____

(3, 5) _____

(2, 2) _____

(6, 4) _____

(1, 9) _____

(5, 1) _____

(1, 7) _____

Probability

Another thinking skill to get your brain in gear is figuring probability. Probability is the likelihood or chance that something will happen. Probability is expressed and written as a ratio.

The probability of tossing heads or tails on a coin is one in two (1:2).

The probability of rolling any number on a die is one in six (1:6).

The probability of getting a red on this spinner is two in four (2:4).

The probability of drawing an ace from a deck of cards is four in fifty-two (4:52).

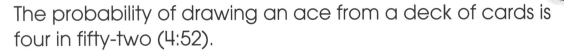

Directions: Write the probability ratios to answer these questions.

1. There are 26 letters in the alphabet. What is the probability of drawing any letter from a set of alphabet cards? _____

2. Five of the 26 alphabet letters are vowels. What is the probability of drawing a vowel from the alphabet cards? _____

3. Matt takes 10 shots at the basketball hoop. Six of his shots are baskets. What is the probability of Matt's next shot being a basket? _____

4. A box contains 10 marbles: 2 white, 3 green, 1 red, 2 orange, and 2 blue. What is the probability of pulling a green marble from the box? _____

   A red marble? _____

5. What is the probability of pulling a marble that is not blue? _____

How Many Outfits?

Directions: Suppose you had two pairs of jeans (one blue and the other gray) and three shirts (orange, red, and green). How many different outfits could you wear? Use a tree diagram to help you with the answer.

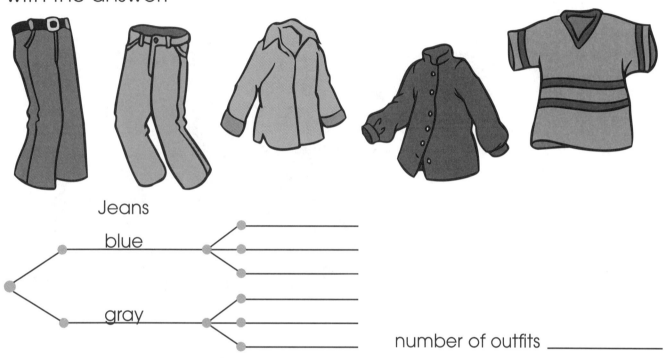

Jeans

blue

gray

number of outfits _____

Directions: Your dad has three shirts and six ties. How many different ways can he wear his shirts and ties? Draw a tree diagram to help you figure out the answer.

number of outfits _____

Name _____

Measurement: Fractions of an Inch

An inch is divided into smaller units, or fractions, of an inch.

Example: This stick of gum is $2\frac{3}{4}$ inches long.

Directions: Use a ruler to measure each line to the nearest quarter of an inch. The first one is done for you.

1. $\frac{3}{4}$ inch _____   _____

2. _____   _____

3. _____   _____

4. _____   _____

5. _____   _____

6. _____   _____

7. _____   _____

$\frac{1}{2}$ Inch

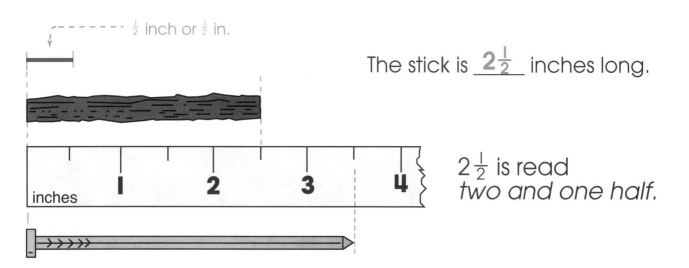

$\frac{1}{2}$ inch or $\frac{1}{2}$ in.

The stick is __2$\frac{1}{2}$__ inches long.

$2\frac{1}{2}$ is read
two and one half.

inches | 1 | 2 | 3 | 4

The nail is _____ inches long.

Directions: Find the length of each picture to the nearest $\frac{1}{2}$ inch.

1. _____ in.

2. _____ in.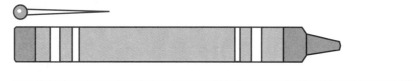

3. _____ in.

4. _____ in.

5. _____ in.

6. _____ in.

Directions: Use a ruler to draw a line segment for each measurement.

7. $1\frac{1}{2}$ in.

8. $3\frac{1}{2}$ in.

9. $4\frac{1}{2}$ in.

10. 5 in.

 Math: Grade 4

Measurement: Foot, Yard, Mile

Directions: Choose the measure of distance you would use for each object.

I foot = 12 inches
I yard = 3 feet
I mile = 1,760 yards or 5,280 feet

   inches

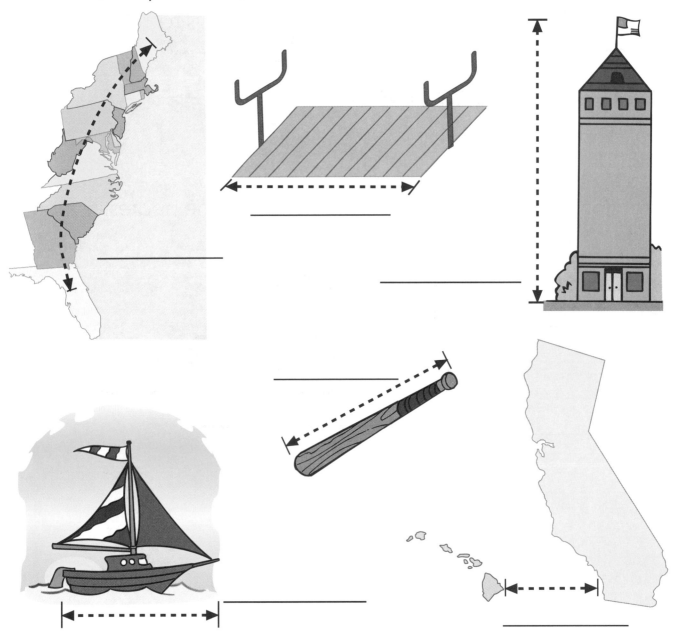

Metric Measurement:
Centimeter, Meter, Kilometer

In the metric system, there are three units of linear measurement: centimeter (cm), meter (m), and kilometer (km).

Centimeters (cm) are used to measure the lengths of small to medium-sized objects. **Meters (m)** measure the lengths of longer objects, such as the width of a swimming pool or height of a tree (100 cm = 1 meter). **Kilometers (km)** measure long distances, such as the distance from Cleveland to Cincinnati or the width of the Atlantic Ocean (1,000 m = 1 km).

Directions: Write whether you would use cm, m, or km to measure each object.

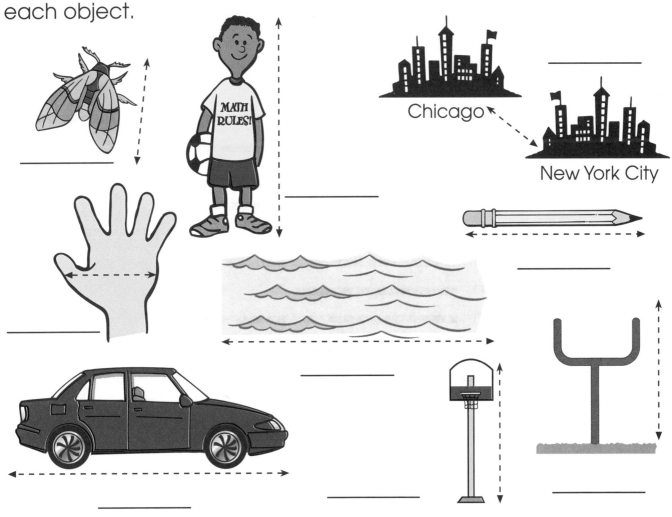

Chicago

New York City

MATH RULES!

Name _____

Millimeter

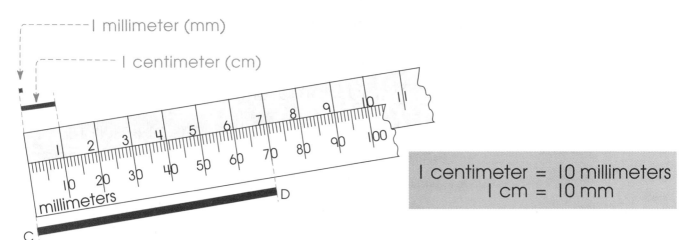

I centimeter = 10 millimeters
I cm = 10 mm

Line segment CD is ____7____ centimeters or _____ millimeters long.

Directions: Solve the problems. Find the length of each line segment to the nearest centimeter. Then, find the length of each line segment to the nearest millimeter.

1. _____ cm   _____ mm
2. _____ cm   _____ mm
3. _____ cm   _____ mm
4. _____ cm   _____ mm

Find the length of each line segment to the nearest millimeter.

5. _____ mm
6. _____ mm
7. _____ mm
8. _____ mm

Use a ruler to draw a line segment for each measurement.

9. 50 mm
10. 80 mm
11. 25 mm
12. 55 mm

Name_____

Units of Length

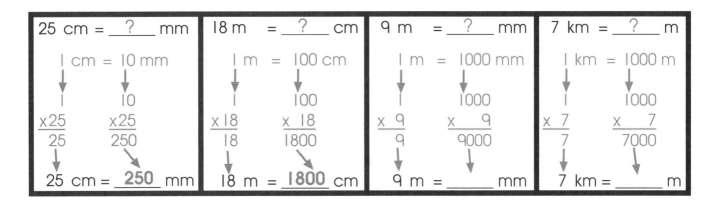

Directions: Complete the following.

9 cm = _____ mm   7 cm = _____ mm

9 m = _____ cm   6 m = _____ cm

9 m = _____ mm   4 m = _____ mm

9 km = _____ m   5 km = _____ m

16 m = _____ cm   8 m = _____ mm

89 km = _____ m   46 m = _____ cm

28 cm = _____ mm   18 km = _____ m

13 m = _____ mm   42 cm = _____ mm

16 m = _____ mm   10 m = _____ cm

10 km = _____ m   25 m = _____ mm

Measurement: Perimeter and Area

Perimeter is the distance around a figure. It is found by adding the lengths of the sides. **Area** is the number of square units needed to cover a region. The area is found by adding the number of square units. A unit can be any unit of measure. Most often, inches, feet, or yards are used.

Directions: Find the perimeter and area for each figure. The first one is done for you.

 = 1 square unit

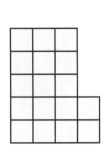

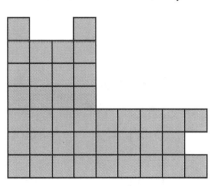

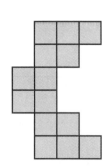

Perimeter = __18__ units

Area = __17__ sq. units

Perimeter = _____ units

Area = _____ sq. units

Perimeter = _____ units

Area = _____ sq. units

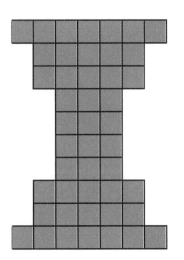

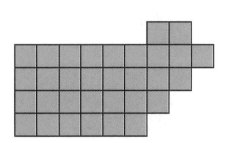

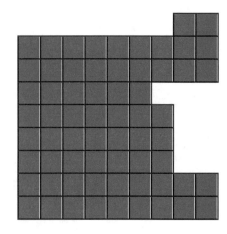

Perimeter = _____ units

Area = _____ sq. units

Perimeter = _____ units

Area = _____ sq. units

Perimeter = _____ units

Area = _____ sq. units

Perimeter

The distance around a figure is called its **perimeter**.

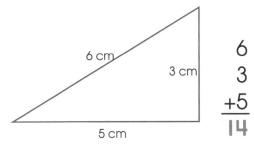

6
3
+5
14

The perimeter is __14__ centimeters.

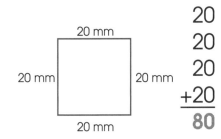

20
20
20
+20
80

The perimeter is __80__ millimeters.

Directions: Solve the problems. Find the perimeter of each figure.

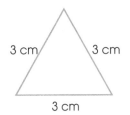

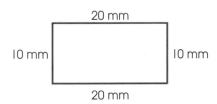

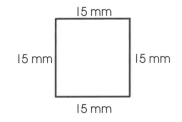

perimeter: _____ cm   perimeter: _____ mm   perimeter: _____ mm

Find the length of each side in centimeters. Then, find the perimeter.

perimeter: _____ cm

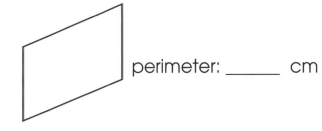

perimeter: _____ cm

Find the length of each side in millimeters. Then, find the perimeter.

perimeter: _____ mm

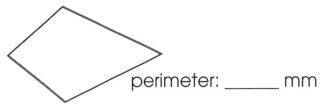

perimeter: _____ mm

Measurement: Volume

Volume is the number of cubic units that fit inside a figure.

Directions: Find the volume of each figure. The first one is done for you.

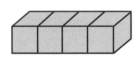

___4___ cubic units

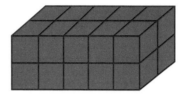

_____ cubic units

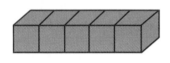

_____ cubic units

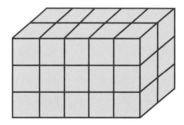

_____ cubic units

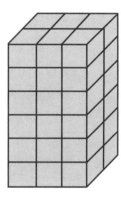

_____ cubic units

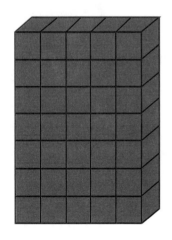

_____ cubic units

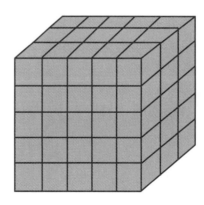

_____ cubic units

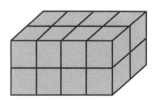

_____ cubic units

Measurement: Volume

The volume of a figure can also be calculated by multiplying the length times the width times the height.
Use the formula: V= l x w x h.

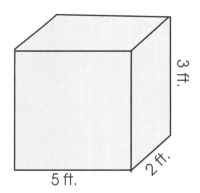

Example:

3 x 5 x 2 = **30 cubic feet**

Directions: Find the volume of the following figures. Label your answers in cubic feet, inches, or yards. The first one is done for you.

6 cubic inches
_____

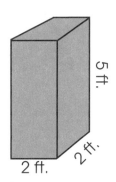

_____

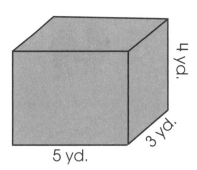

_____

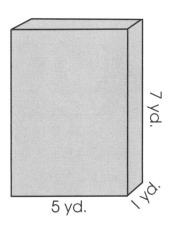

_____

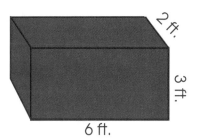

_____

Measurement: Ounce, Pound, Ton

The **ounce**, **pound**, and **ton** are units in the standard system for measuring weight.

Directions: Choose the measure of weight you would use for each object.

16 ounces = 1 pound
2,000 pounds = 1 ton

       ounce   **pound**   **ton**

Example: ounces _____    _____

 _____    _____

 _____    _____

 _____    _____

Metric Measurement: Gram and Kilogram

Grams and **kilograms** are measurements of weight in the metric system. A gram (g) weighs about $\frac{1}{28}$ of an ounce. A grape or paper clip weighs about one gram. There are 1,000 grams in a kilogram. A kilogram (kg) weighs about 2.2 pounds. A brick weighs about 1 kilogram.

Directions: Choose grams or kilograms to measure the following.

Example:

grams
_____

_____

_____

_____

_____

_____

_____

_____

_____

Name _____

Time Problems

Directions: Draw the hands on the clocks to show the starting time and the ending time. Then, write the answer to the question.

1. The bike race started at 2:55 P.M. and lasted 2 hours and 10 minutes. What time did the race end?

_____

4. Sherry walked in the 12-mile Hunger Walk. She started at 12:30 P.M. and finished at 4:50 P.M. How long did she walk?

_____

2. The 500-mile auto race started at 11:00 A.M. and lasted 2 hours and 25 minutes. What time did the race end?

_____

5. The chili cook-off started at 10:00 A.M., and all the chili was cooked by 4:30 P.M. How long did it take to cook the chili?

_____

3. The train left Indianapolis at 7:25 A.M. and arrived in Chicago at 10:50 A.M. How long did the trip take?

_____

6. The chili judging began at 4:30 P.M. After 3 hours and 45 minutes the chili had all been eaten. At what time was the chili judging finished?

_____

Money

1 cent = 1¢ or $0.01
3 cents = __3¢__ or _$0.03_
65 cents = __65¢__ or _$0.65_
6 cents = __6¢__ or $ _0.06_
98 cents = __98¢__ or $ _0.98_

1 dollar = $1.00
3 dollars and 2 cents = _$3.02_
4 dollars and 59 cents = _$4.59_
6 dollars and 3 cents = _$6.03_
5 dollars and 72 cents = _$5.72_

Directions: Complete the following.

5 cents = _____¢	25¢ = $_____	$0.83 = _____¢
10 cents = $_____	50¢ = $_____	$0.04 = _____¢
25 cents = _____¢	75¢ = $_____	$0.29 = _____¢
50 cents = $_____	10¢ = $_____	$0.06 = _____¢
85 cents = _____¢	95¢ = $_____	$0.60 = _____¢
100 cents = $_____	5¢ = $_____	$0.99 = _____¢

Directions: Complete the following.

4 dollars and 8 cents = $_____
7 dollars and 63 cents = $_____
3 dollars and 9 cents = $_____
6 dollars and 19 cents = $_____
5 dollars and 79 cents = $_____
18 dollars and 75 cents = $_____

$6.25 = 6 dollars and _____ cents
$3.75 = _____ dollars and 75 cents
$7.05 = 7 dollars and _____ cents
$9.65 = _____ dollars and 65 cents
$4.19 = _____ dollars and _____ cents
$8.69 = _____ dollars and _____ cents

Name _____

Money

Add the numbers.

```
  25¢        $0.85
  45¢         2.08
+ 19¢       + 3.76
─────       ──────
  89¢        $6.69
```

Subtract the numbers.

```
  72¢        $12.07
- 26¢       -  4.83
─────       ───────
  46¢         $7.24
```

Write ¢ or $ and a decimal point in the answer.

Write ¢ or $ and a decimal point in the answer.

Directions: Add or subtract.

```
   2 3¢          4 7¢         $0.4 6        $5.4 7        $3 6.9 5
 + 4 4¢        + 2 5¢        + 0.7 3       + 8.2 1       + 7 2.0 2
 ───────       ───────       ───────       ───────       ─────────
     ¢
```

```
   7 9¢          5 6¢         $1.2 7        $4.6 7        $3 6.7 8
 - 2 3¢        - 2 7¢        - 0.5 3       - 2.8 9       - 2 7.9 0
 ───────       ───────       ───────       ───────       ─────────
```

```
   1 4¢            6¢         $0.5 7        $5.2 5        $1 6.9 6
 + 7 1¢        + 8 7¢        + 0.6 8       + 9.4 6       + 2 7.4 5
 ───────       ───────       ───────       ───────       ─────────
```

```
   8 8¢          9 2¢         $2.6 4        $6.2 7        $4 9.7 8
 - 6 9¢        - 8 9¢        - 0.5 7       - 2.8 9       - 1 8.8 9
 ───────       ───────       ───────       ───────       ─────────
```

```
   1 2¢          4 3¢         $0.7 5        $0.1 2        $4 7.5 2
   3 9¢          2 7¢          0.6 5         4.6 9         8 9.2 5
 + 2 4¢        + 2 6¢        + 0.9 7       + 5.8 7       + 6 7.4 7
 ───────       ───────       ───────       ───────       ─────────
```

```
  $2.4 6        $1.5 7        $3.0 7        $7.0 0        $6 0.4 7
 - 0.8 7       - 0.9 9       - 1.8 5       - 2.4 8       - 2 7.5 9
 ───────       ───────       ───────       ───────       ─────────
```

Fast Food

Mealwormy is the latest restaurant of that famous fast food creator, Buggs I. Lyke. His Mealwormy Burger costs $1.69. An order of Roasted Roaches cost $0.59 for the regular size and $0.79 for the larger size. A Cricket Cola is $0.89.

Directions: Solve the problems.

1. You buy a Mealwormy Burger and a regular order of Roasted Roaches. What is the total?

2. Your teacher buys a Cricket Cola and a regular order of Roasted Roaches. What does it cost her?

3. Your mom goes to Mealwormy to buy your dinner. She spends $3.37. How much change does she get from a $5.00 bill?

4. Your best friend orders a Mealwormy Burger, a large order of Roasted Roaches, and Cricket Cola. How much will it cost?

5. The principal is very hungry, so his bill comes to $14.37. How much change will he get from $20.00?

6. You have $1.17 in your bank. How much more do you need to pay for a Mealwormy Burger?

Math: Grade 4

Multiplying Money

Money is multiplied in the same way other numbers are. The only difference is a dollar sign and a decimal point are added to the final product.

Directions: Follow the steps, then multiply these problems.

Steps:

1. Multiply by ones.
   1. 4 x 8 = 32 (Carry the 3.)
   2. 4 x 2 = 8 + 3 = 11
      (Carry the 1.)
   3. 4 x 4 = 16 + 1 = 17

$$
\begin{array}{r}
{}^{1\ 3}\ \ \\
\$4.28 \\
\times\quad 34 \\
\hline
1712
\end{array}
\qquad
\begin{array}{r}
\$3.42 \\
\times\quad 25 \\
\hline
\end{array}
\qquad
\begin{array}{r}
\$5.42 \\
\times\quad 61 \\
\hline
\end{array}
$$

2. 1. Cross out the carried digits.
   2. Add the zero.

$$
\begin{array}{r}
\cancel{\times}\cancel{\times} \\
\$4.28 \\
\times\quad 34 \\
\hline
1712 \\
0
\end{array}
$$

3. Multiply by tens.
   1. 3 x 8 = 24
      (Carry the 2.)
   2. 3 x 2 = 6 + 2 = 8
   3. 3 x 4 = 12

$$
\begin{array}{r}
{}^{2}\ \ \\
\$4.28 \\
\times\quad 34 \\
\hline
1712 \\
12840
\end{array}
\qquad
\begin{array}{r}
\$3.81 \\
\times\quad 46 \\
\hline
\end{array}
\qquad
\begin{array}{r}
\$8.20 \\
\times\quad 55 \\
\hline
\end{array}
$$

4. Add.
   1,712 + 12,840 = 14,552

$$
\begin{array}{r}
\$4.28 \\
\times\quad 34 \\
\hline
1712 \\
+12840 \\
\hline
14,552
\end{array}
$$

5. Add the dollar sign and the decimal point.

$$
\begin{array}{r}
\$4.28 \\
\times\quad 34 \\
\hline
1712 \\
+12840 \\
\hline
\$145.52
\end{array}
\qquad
\begin{array}{r}
\$9.42 \\
\times\quad 31 \\
\hline
\end{array}
\qquad
\begin{array}{r}
\$4.23 \\
\times\quad 96 \\
\hline
\end{array}
$$

Money Math

Directions: Solve these problems. Remember the decimal point and dollar sign in your answers.

$3.42
x   27

$2.45
x   34

$6.42
x   56

$8.43
x   30

$0.49
x   56

$2.53
x   41

$8.21
x   37

$4.21
x   36

$5.41
x   42

$0.21
x   84

$0.89
x   32

$4.25
x   31

Too Much Information

Directions: Cross out the information not needed and solve the problems.

1. All 20 of the students from Sandy's class went to the movies. Tickets cost $3.50 each. Drinks cost $0.95 each. How much altogether did the students spend on tickets?

2. Five students had ice cream, 12 others had candy. Ice cream cost $0.75 per cup. How much did the students spend on ice cream?

3. Seven of the 20 students did not like the movie. Three of the 20 students had seen the movie before. How many students had not seen the movie before?

4. Six of the students spent a total of $16.50 for refreshments and $21.00 for their tickets. How much did each spend for refreshments?

5. Of the students, 11 were girls and 9 were boys. At $1.50 per ticket, how much did the boys' tickets cost altogether?

6. Mary paid $0.95 for an orange drink and $0.65 for a candy bar. Sarah paid $2.50 for popcorn. How much did Mary's refreshments cost her?

7. Ten of the students went back to see the movie again the next day. Each student paid $3.50 for a ticket, $2.50 for popcorn, and $0.95 for a soft drink. How much did each student pay?

Name _____

Perplexing Problems

Directions: Solve these problems.

1. Mark, David, Curt, and Jordan rented a motorized skateboard for 1 hour. What was the cost for each of them—split equally 4 ways?

Total:
$17.36 $ _____

4. Five students pitched in to buy Mr. Foley a birthday gift. How much did each of them contribute?

Total:
$9.60 $ _____

2. Mary, Cheryl, and Betty went to the skating rink. What was their individual cost?

Total:
$7.44 $ _____

5. Carol, Katelyn, and Kimberly bought lunch at their favorite salad shop. What did each of them pay for lunch?

Total:
$12.63 $ _____

7. Debbie, Sarah, Michele, and Kelly earned $6.56 altogether collecting cans. How much did each of them earn individually?

Total:
$6.56 $ _____

3. Five friends went to the Hot Spot Café for lunch. They all ordered the special. What did it cost?

Total:
$27.45 $ _____

6. Lee and Ricardo purchased an awesome model rocket together. What was the cost for each of them?

Total:
$9.52 $ _____

8. The total fee for Erik, Bill, and Steve to enter the science museum was $8.76. What amount did each of them pay?

Total:
$8.76 $ _____

Answer Key

Place Value

Place value is the value of a digit, or numeral, shown by where it is in the number. For example, in 1,234, **1** has the place value of thousands, **2** is hundreds, **3** is tens, and **4** is ones.

Directions: Write the numbers in the correct boxes to find how far the car has traveled.

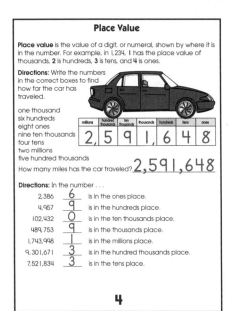

one thousand
six hundreds
eight ones
nine ten thousands
four tens
two millions
five hundred thousands

millions	hundred thousands	ten thousands	thousands	hundreds	tens	ones
2,	5	9	1,	6	4	8

How many miles has the car traveled? **2,591,648**

Directions: In the number . . .

2,386	**6**	is in the ones place.
4,957	**9**	is in the hundreds place.
102,432	**0**	is in the ten thousands place.
489,753	**9**	is in the thousands place.
1,743,998	**1**	is in the millions place.
9,301,671	**3**	is in the hundred thousands place.
7,521,834	**3**	is in the tens place.

4

Place Value: Expanded Notation and Standard Form

Directions: Use the number cube or spinner to create numbers for the place value boxes below. Then, write the number in expanded notation and standard form.

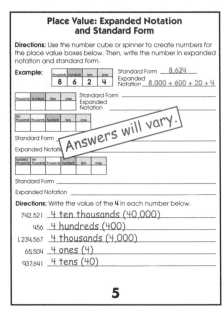

Example:

thousands	hundreds	tens	ones
8	6	2	4

Standard Form ___8,624___
Expanded Notation ___8,000 + 600 + 20 + 4___

Answers will vary.

Standard Form _____
Expanded Notation _____

Standard Form _____
Expanded Notation _____

Standard Form _____
Expanded Notation _____

Directions: Write the value of the **4** in each number below.

742,521	**4 ten thousands (40,000)**
456	**4 hundreds (400)**
1,234,567	**4 thousands (4,000)**
65,504	**4 ones (4)**
937,641	**4 tens (40)**

5

Addition

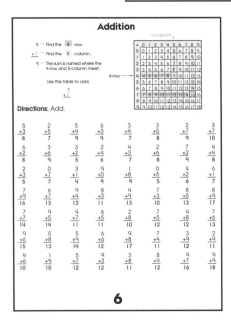

4 — Find the **4**-row.
+5 — Find the **5**-column.
— The sum is named where the 4-row and 5-column meet.

Use the table to add.
7
+5

Directions: Add.

5 +3 = 8	2 +5 = 7	5 +4 = 9	6 +3 = 9	3 +4 = 7	3 +5 = 8	3 +2 = 5	2 +7 = 9	3 +7 = 10
6 +2 = 8	3 +6 = 9	3 +2 = 5	2 +4 = 6	4 +3 = 7	2 +6 = 8	7 +2 = 9	4 +4 = 8	
2 +3 = 5	0 +7 = 7	3 +1 = 4	9 +0 = 9	1 +8 = 9	0 +5 = 5	4 +2 = 6	6 +1 = 7	
7 +9 = 16	6 +7 = 13	4 +4 = 8	8 +3 = 11	4 +9 = 13	7 +3 = 10	8 +5 = 13	8 +9 = 17	
7 +7 = 14	9 +5 = 14	3 +8 = 11	6 +5 = 11	2 +8 = 10	7 +5 = 12	4 +8 = 12	7 +6 = 13	
9 +6 = 15	5 +8 = 13	5 +9 = 14	9 +6 = 15	9 +8 = 17	7 +4 = 11	3 +9 = 12	2 +9 = 11	
4 +6 = 10	1 +9 = 10	5 +7 = 12	9 +3 = 12	3 +8 = 11	8 +4 = 12	9 +7 = 16	9 +9 = 18	

6

Leafy Addition

Directions: Add, then color according to the code.

Code:
green — 79   orange — 35   red — 78
yellow — 87   purple — 56   brown — 94

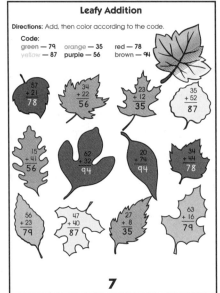

57 +21 = 78
34 +22 = 56
23 +12 = 35
35 +52 = 87
15 +41 = 56
62 +32 = 94
20 +74 = 94
34 +44 = 78
56 +23 = 79
47 +40 = 87
27 + 8 = 35
63 +16 = 79

7

Adding Larger Numbers

When adding two-, three-, and four-digit numbers, add the ones first, then tens, hundreds, thousands, and so on.

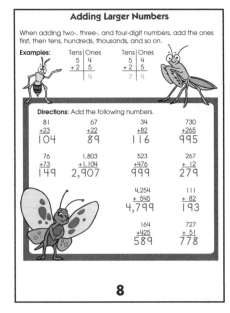

Examples:

Tens	Ones
5	4
+2	5
	9

Tens	Ones
5	4
+2	5
7	9

Directions: Add the following numbers.

81 +23 = 104	67 +22 = 89	34 +82 = 116	730 +265 = 995
76 +73 = 149	1,803 +1,104 = 2,907	523 +476 = 999	267 + 12 = 279
		4,254 + 545 = 4,799	111 + 82 = 193
		164 +425 = 589	727 + 51 = 778

8

Subtraction

Subtraction is "taking away" or subtracting one number from another.

Directions: Complete the following problems as quickly and as accurately as you can.

18 - 9 = 9	13 - 6 = 7	12 - 5 = 7	17 - 8 = 9	16 - 8 = 8
12 - 5 = 7	10 - 4 = 6	5 - 3 = 2	14 - 6 = 8	15 - 9 = 6
9 - 5 = 4	8 - 3 = 5	6 - 2 = 4	5 - 4 = 1	10 - 7 = 3
11 - 4 = 7	12 - 8 = 4	16 - 9 = 7	11 - 8 = 3	10 -10 = 0

How quickly did you complete this page? **Answers will vary.**

9

Subtraction: Regrouping

Directions: Subtract using regrouping.

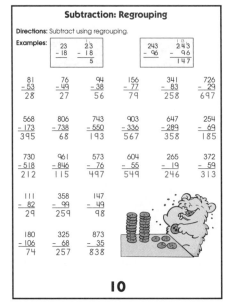

Examples:

23	2³ -18 = 5		243	2⁴³ - 96 = 147
-18			- 96	

81 - 53 = 28	76 - 49 = 27	94 - 38 = 56	156 - 77 = 79	341 - 83 = 258	726 - 29 = 697
568 - 173 = 395	806 - 738 = 68	743 - 550 = 193	903 - 336 = 567	647 - 289 = 358	254 - 69 = 185
730 - 518 = 212	961 - 846 = 115	573 - 76 = 497	604 - 55 = 549	265 - 19 = 246	372 - 59 = 313
111 - 82 = 29	358 - 99 = 259	147 - 49 = 98			
180 - 106 = 74	325 - 68 = 257	873 - 35 = 838			

10

Addition and Subtraction

Directions: Add or subtract, using regrouping when needed.

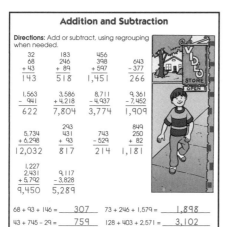

32 68 + 43 **143**	183 246 + 89 **518**	456 398 + 597 **1,451**	643 – 377 **266**
1,563 – 941 **622**	3,586 + 4,218 **7,804**	8,711 – 4,937 **3,774**	9,361 – 7,452 **1,909**
5,734 + 6,298 **12,032**	293 431 + 93 **817**	743 – 529 **214**	849 250 + 82 **1,181**
1,227 2,431 + 5,792 **9,450**	9,117 – 3,828 **5,289**		

68 + 93 + 146 = **307**   73 + 246 + 1,579 = **1,898**

43 + 745 – 29 = **759**   128 + 403 + 2,571 = **3,102**

156 + 627 + 541 = **1,324**   97 + 51 + 37 + 79 = **264**

Tom walks 389 steps from his house to the video store. It is 149 steps to Elm Street. It is 52 steps from Maple Street to the video store. How many steps is it from Elm Street to Maple Street? **188 steps**

11

Rounding: Tens

Rounding a number means expressing it to the nearest ten, hundred, thousand, and so on. Knowing how to round numbers makes estimating sums, differences, and products easier. When rounding to the nearest ten, the key number is in the ones place. If the ones digit is **5** or larger, round up to the next highest ten. If the ones digit is **4** or less, round down to the nearest ten.

Examples:
- Round 81 to the nearest ten.
- **1** is the key digit.
- If it is less than **5**, round down.
- Answer: <u>80</u>
- Round 246 to the nearest ten.
- **6** is the key digit.
- If it is more than **5**, round up.
- Answer: <u>250</u>

Directions: Round these numbers to the nearest ten.

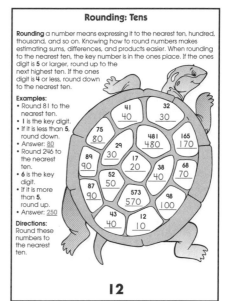

41 **40** 32 **30** 75 **80** 481 **480** 165 **170** 89 **90** 30 **30** 17 **20** 38 **40** 68 **70** 52 **50** 87 **90** 573 **570** 98 **100** 43 **40** 12 **10**

12

Rounding: Hundreds and Thousands

When rounding to the nearest hundred, the key number is in the tens place. If the tens digit is **5** or larger, round up to nearest hundred. If the tens digit is **4** or less, round down to the nearest hundred.

Examples:
Round 871 to the nearest hundred.
7 is the key digit.
If it is more than **5**, round up.
Answer: <u>900</u>

Round 421 to the nearest hundred.
2 is the key digit.
If it is less than **4**, round down.
Answer: <u>400</u>

Directions: Round these numbers to the nearest hundred.

255 **300**   368 **400**   443 **400**   578 **600**

562 **600**   698 **700**   99 **100**   775 **800**

812 **800**   592 **600**   124 **100**   10,235 **10,200**

When rounding to the nearest thousand, the key number is in the hundreds place. If the hundreds digit is **5** or larger, round up to the nearest thousand. If the hundreds digit is **4** or less, round down to the nearest thousand.

Examples:
Round 7,932 to the nearest thousand.
9 is the key digit.
If it is more than **5**, round up.
Answer: <u>8,000</u>

Round 1,368 to the nearest thousand.
3 is the key digit.
If it is less than **4**, round down.
Answer: <u>1,000</u>

Directions: Round these numbers to the nearest thousand.

8,631 **9,000**   1,248 **1,000**   798 **1,000**

999 **1,000**   6,229 **6,000**   8,461 **8,000**

9,654 **10,000**   4,963 **5,000**   99,923 **100,000**

13

Rounding

Directions: Round these numbers to the nearest ten.

18 **20**   33 **30**   82 **80**   56 **60**

24 **20**   49 **50**   91 **90**   67 **70**

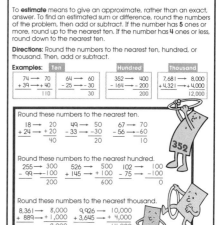

Directions: Round these numbers to the nearest hundred.

243 **200**   689 **700**   263 **300**   162 **200**

389 **400**   720 **700**   351 **400**   490 **500**

463 **500**   846 **800**   928 **900**   733 **700**

Directions: Round these numbers to the nearest thousand.

2,638 **3,000**   3,940 **4,000**   8,653 **9,000**

6,238 **6,000**   1,429 **1,000**   5,061 **5,000**

7,289 **7,000**   2,742 **3,000**   9,460 **9,000**

3,109 **3,000**   4,697 **5,000**   8,302 **8,000**

Directions: Round these numbers to the nearest ten thousand.

11,368 **10,000**   38,421 **40,000**

75,302 **80,000**   67,932 **70,000**

14,569 **10,000**   49,906 **50,000**

93,694 **90,000**   81,648 **80,000**

26,784 **30,000**   87,065 **90,000**

57,843 **60,000**   29,399 **30,000**

14

Estimating

To **estimate** means to give an approximate, rather than an exact, answer. To find an estimated sum or difference, round the numbers of the problem, then add or subtract. If the number has **5** ones or more, round up to the nearest ten. If the number has **4** ones or less, round down to the nearest ten.

Directions: Round the numbers to the nearest ten, hundred, or thousand. Then, add or subtract.

Examples:

Ten	Hundred	Thousand
74 → 70 + 39 → + 40 **110**	64 → 60 – 25 → – 30 **30**	352 → 400 – 164 → – 200 **200**	7,681 → 8,000 + 4,321 → + 4,000 **12,000**

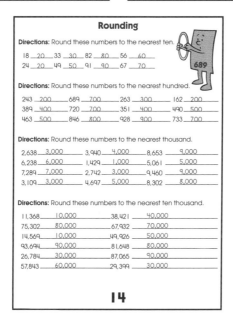

Round these numbers to the nearest ten.

18 → **20**   49 → **50**   67 → **70**
+ 24 → + **20**   – 33 → – **30**   – 56 → – **60**
40   **10**   **10**

Round these numbers to the nearest hundred.

255 → **300**   526 → **500**   102 → **100**
– 99 → – **100**   + 145 → + **100**   – 75 → – **100**
200   **600**   **0**

Round these numbers to the nearest thousand.

8,361 → **8,000**   9,926 → **10,000**
+ 889 → + **1,000**   + 3,645 → + **4,000**
9,000   **14,000**

15

Skip Counting

Skip counting is a quick way to count by skipping numbers. For example, when you skip count by 2s, you count **2, 4, 6, 8,** and so on. You can skip count by many different numbers such as **2s, 4s, 5s, 10s,** and **100s.**

The illustration below shows skip counting by **2s** to 14.

Directions: Use the number line to help you skip count by **2s** from **0** to **20.**

0, **2**, **4**, **6**, 8, **10**, **12**, 14, **16**, **18**, **20**

Directions: Skip count by **3s** by filling in the rocks across the pond.

3   **6**   **9**   **12**   **15**   **18**   **21**

16

Multiplication Facts

5 → Find the **5**-row.
× 6 → Find the **6**-column.
30 → The product is named where the 5-row and 6-column meet.

Use the table to multiply.

7
× 9

Directions: Multiply.

6 ×1 **6**	7 ×8 **56**	8 ×9 **72**	9 ×0 **0**	7 ×7 **49**	6 ×7 **42**	7 ×1 **7**	4 ×6 **24**
9 ×9 **81**	6 ×2 **12**	7 ×6 **42**	9 ×1 **9**	1 ×1 **1**	6 ×8 **48**	8 ×8 **64**	3 ×7 **21**
8 ×0 **0**	7 ×5 **35**	6 ×0 **0**	9 ×2 **18**	8 ×7 **56**	6 ×9 **54**	7 ×0 **0**	4 ×7 **28**
5 ×6 **30**	9 ×3 **27**	7 ×4 **28**	6 ×3 **18**	9 ×4 **36**	8 ×4 **32**	8 ×6 **48**	3 ×6 **18**
7 ×9 **63**	5 ×7 **35**	5 ×8 **40**	8 ×5 **40**	6 ×4 **24**	7 ×3 **21**	9 ×5 **45**	2 ×6 **12**
7 ×2 **14**	8 ×4 **32**	9 ×6 **54**	9 ×7 **63**	9 ×4 **30**	6 ×5 **30**	9 ×8 **72**	2 ×8 **16**
8 ×3 **24**	5 ×9 **45**	3 ×8 **24**	8 ×2 **16**	3 ×9 **27**	2 ×7 **14**	6 ×6 **36**	2 ×9 **18**

17

Fact Factory

Factors are the numbers multiplied together in a multiplication problem. The **product** is the answer.

Directions: Write the missing factors or products.

x	5
1	5
5	25
4	20
6	30
3	15
2	10
7	35
3	18
9	45

x	9
8	72
3	27
4	36
9	81
6	54
7	63
2	18
1	9

x	7
2	14
5	35
6	42
8	56
7	49
4	28
3	21
0	0

x	3
7	21
4	12
6	18
3	9
2	6
5	15
6	6
8	24

x	1
1	1
12	12
10	10
3	3
5	5
7	7
6	6
4	4

x	8
9	72
8	64
4	32
5	40
6	48
7	56
3	24
2	16

x	2
12	24
1	2
11	22
2	4
10	20
1	2
3	6
9	18
4	8

x	4
2	8
4	16
6	24
8	32
3	12
1	4
3	12
5	20
7	28

x	6
7	42
6	36
5	30
4	24
3	18
2	12
1	6
0	0

x	10
2	20
3	30
4	40
5	50
6	60
7	70
8	80
9	90

x	11
4	44
7	77
9	99
10	110
3	33
5	55
6	66
8	88

x	12
1	12
2	24
3	36
4	48
5	60
6	72
7	84
8	96

Multiplication

$$4 \times 2 = 8 \qquad 40 \times 2 = 80$$
If $2 \times 4 = 8$, then $2 \times 40 = 80$.

Multiply 3 ones by 2. $43 \times 2 = 6$
Multiply 4 tens by 2. $43 \times 2 = 86$

Directions: Multiply.

3 ×3 = 9	30 ×3 = 90	2 ×4 = 8	20 ×4 = 80	3 ×2 = 6	30 ×2 = 60
2 ×3 = 6	30 ×3 = 90	32 ×3 = 96	1 ×2 = 2	40 ×2 = 80	41 ×2 = 82
11 ×9 = 99	33 ×3 = 99	12 ×3 = 36	14 ×2 = 28	31 ×3 = 93	13 ×3 = 39
32 ×2 = 64	23 ×3 = 69	42 ×2 = 84	21 ×4 = 84	13 ×2 = 26	11 ×6 = 66
12 ×2 = 24	11 ×5 = 55	33 ×2 = 66	11 ×3 = 33	21 ×2 = 42	22 ×3 = 66
11 ×4 = 44	44 ×2 = 88	22 ×2 = 44	11 ×8 = 88	11 ×2 = 22	13 ×2 = 26
23 ×2 = 46	22 ×4 = 88	24 ×2 = 48	21 ×3 = 63	31 ×2 = 62	11 ×7 = 77

Multiplying and Regrouping

1. Multiply 3 x 8 in the ones column. Ask: Do I need to regroup?

2. Multiply 3 x 3 in the tens column. Add the 2 you carried over from the ones column. Ask: Do I need to regroup?

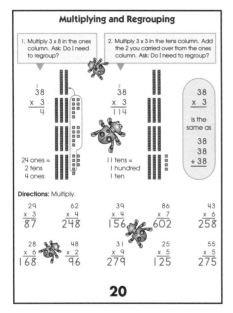

$38 \times 3 \rightarrow 4$ (carry 2)

$38 \times 3 = 114$

38×3 is the same as
$$38 + 38 + 38$$

24 ones = 2 tens 4 ones

11 tens = 1 hundred 1 ten

Directions: Multiply.

29 ×3 = 87	62 ×4 = 248	39 ×4 = 156	86 ×7 = 602	43 ×6 = 258
28 ×6 = 168	48 ×2 = 96	31 ×9 = 279	25 ×5 = 125	55 ×5 = 275

21

Hmm, What Should I Do?

Examples: $52 + 9 = 61$ $37 - 8 = 29$
$8 \times 4 = 32$ $28 \div 7 = 4$

Directions: Write the correct symbols in the circles.

$7 \times 8 = 56$	$81 - 6 = 75$	$55 - 3 = 52$
$54 \div 9 = 6$	$2 \times 1 = 2$	$40 - 2 = 38$
$36 - 5 = 31$	$0 + 2 = 2$	$8 \times 8 = 64$
$12 + 6 = 18$	$9 \times 8 = 72$	$18 + 5 = 23$
$72 - 7 = 65$		$32 + 5 = 37$
$0 \times 1 = 0$		$48 \div 6 = 8$
$9 \times 1 = 9$		$32 \div 4 = 8$
$45 \div 9 = 5$		$6 \times 7 = 42$

22

Multiplication: Tens, Hundreds, Thousands

When multiplying a number by **10**, the answer is the number with a **0**. It is like counting by tens.

Examples:

10 ×1 = 10	10 ×2 = 20	10 ×3 = 30	10 ×4 = 40	10 ×5 = 50	10 ×6 = 60

When multiplying a number by **100**, the answer is a number with two **0s**. When multiplying by **1,000**, the answer is a number with three **0s**.

Examples:

100 ×1 = 100	100 ×2 = 200	100 ×3 = 300	1,000 ×1 = 1,000	1,000 ×2 = 2,000	1,000 ×3 = 3,000
4 ×6 = 24	400 ×6 = 2,400	800 ×3 = 2,400	7 ×5 = 35	700 ×5 = 3,500	

Directions: Multiply.

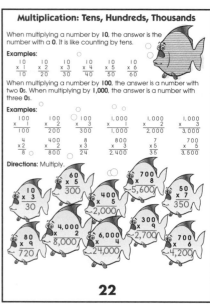

60 ×5 = 300
10 ×3 = 30
700 ×8 = 5,600
50 ×7 = 350
400 ×5 = 2,000
80 ×9 = 720
4,000 ×2 = 8,000
6,000 ×4 = 24,000
300 ×9 = 2,700
700 ×6 = 4,200

Multiplication: Two-Digit Numbers Times Two-Digit Numbers

Follow the steps for multiplying a two-digit number by a two-digit number using regrouping.

Example:

Step 1: Multiply the ones. Regroup.
$$63 \times 68 = 504$$

Step 2: Multiply the tens. Regroup. Add.
$$63 \times 68 \rightarrow 3,780$$
$$504 + 3,780 = 4,284$$

Directions: Multiply.

12 ×55 = 660	27 ×15 = 405	65 ×27 = 1,755	19 ×39 = 741	99 ×13 = 1,287	35 ×14 = 490
43 ×26 = 1,118	38 ×17 = 646	53 ×86 = 4,558	47 ×72 = 3,384	57 ×62 = 3,534	48 ×33 = 1,584
27 ×54 = 1,458	93 ×45 = 4,185	64 ×16 = 1,024	53 ×23 = 1,219		

The Jones farm has 24 cows that each produce 52 quarts of milk a day. How many quarts are produced each day altogether?   **1,248 quarts**

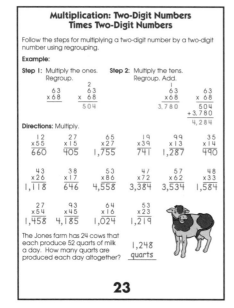

Multiplication: Three-Digit Numbers Times Three-Digit Numbers

Directions: Multiply. Regroup when needed.

Example:
$$563 \times 248$$
$$4,504$$
$$22,520$$
$$+112,600$$
$$139,624$$

Hint: When multiplying by the tens, start writing the number in the tens place. When multiplying by the hundreds, start in the hundreds place.

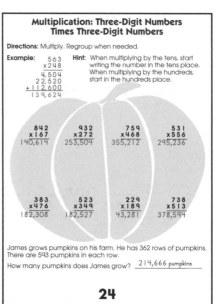

842 ×167 = 140,614	932 ×272 = 253,504	759 ×468 = 355,212	531 ×556 = 295,236
383 ×476 = 182,308	523 ×349 = 182,527	229 ×189 = 43,281	738 ×513 = 378,594

James grows pumpkins on his farm. He has 362 rows of pumpkins. There are 593 pumpkins in each row.
How many pumpkins does James grow?   **214,666 pumpkins**

Division

Division is a way to find out how many times one number is contained in another number. For example, 28 ÷ 7 = 4 means that there are 4 groups of 7 in 28.

Division problems can be written two ways: 36 ÷ 6 = 6 or $6\overline{)36}$

These are the parts of a division problem:

dividend → 36 ÷ 6 = 6 ← quotient
divisor

divisor → $6\overline{)36}$ ← quotient, dividend

Directions: Divide.

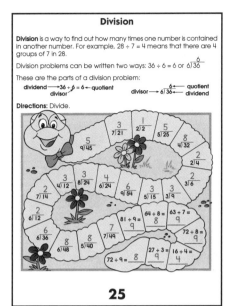

25

Division Facts

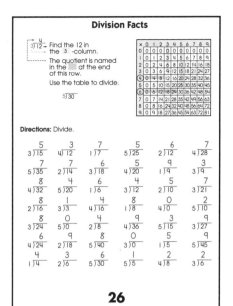

Find the 12 in the 3-column. The quotient is named in the ▓ at the end of this row.
Use the table to divide.

$5\overline{)30}$

Directions: Divide.

$3\overline{)15}$	$4\overline{)12}$	$1\overline{)7}$	$5\overline{)12}$	$2\overline{)12}$	$4\overline{)28}$
$5\overline{)35}$	$2\overline{)14}$	$3\overline{)18}$	$4\overline{)20}$	$1\overline{)9}$	$3\overline{)9}$
$4\overline{)32}$	$5\overline{)20}$	$1\overline{)6}$	$3\overline{)12}$	$2\overline{)10}$	$3\overline{)21}$
$2\overline{)16}$	$3\overline{)3}$	$4\overline{)16}$	$1\overline{)8}$	$4\overline{)0}$	$5\overline{)10}$
$3\overline{)24}$	$5\overline{)0}$	$2\overline{)8}$	$4\overline{)36}$	$5\overline{)15}$	$3\overline{)27}$
$4\overline{)24}$	$2\overline{)18}$	$5\overline{)40}$	$3\overline{)0}$	$1\overline{)5}$	$5\overline{)45}$
$1\overline{)4}$	$2\overline{)6}$	$5\overline{)30}$	$5\overline{)5}$	$4\overline{)8}$	$3\overline{)6}$

26

Two-Digit Quotients

Directions: Follow the steps below. Then divide.

1. Ask: Is the tens digit large enough to divide into? (Yes.) Divide. Multiply the partial quotient (2) by the divisor (4) and subtract from the partial dividend (8).

8 tens divided into 4 groups. How many are in each group? (2)

2. Carry down the 4 in the ones column. Ask: How many groups of 4 are there in 4? (1) Divide. Multiply the partial quotient (1) by the divisor (4) and subtract from the partial dividend (4).

3. When 84 things are divided into 4 groups, there will be 21 in each group.

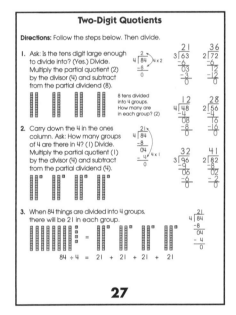

84 ÷ 4 = 21 + 21 + 21 + 21

$3\overline{)63}$	$2\overline{)72}$
$4\overline{)48}$	$2\overline{)56}$
$3\overline{)96}$	$2\overline{)82}$

27

Division Facts

$\begin{array}{r}5\\ \times 6\\ \hline 30\end{array}$ ÷ $6\overline{)30}$ $\begin{array}{r}5\\ \times 7\\ \hline 35\end{array}$ ÷ $7\overline{)35}$

6 × 5 = 30, so 30 ÷ 6 = __5__   7 × 5 = 35, so 35 ÷ 7 = __5__

Directions: Complete the following.

$\begin{array}{r}6\\ \times 6\\ \hline 36\end{array}$ so $6\overline{)36}$ $\begin{array}{r}7\\ \times 6\\ \hline 42\end{array}$ so $6\overline{)42}$ $\begin{array}{r}8\\ \times 6\\ \hline 48\end{array}$ so $6\overline{)48}$ $\begin{array}{r}9\\ \times 6\\ \hline 54\end{array}$ so $6\overline{)54}$

$\begin{array}{r}6\\ \times 7\\ \hline 42\end{array}$ so $7\overline{)42}$ $\begin{array}{r}7\\ \times 7\\ \hline 49\end{array}$ so $7\overline{)49}$ $\begin{array}{r}8\\ \times 7\\ \hline 56\end{array}$ so $7\overline{)56}$ $\begin{array}{r}9\\ \times 7\\ \hline 63\end{array}$ so $7\overline{)63}$

Directions: Divide.

$6\overline{)54}$	$7\overline{)14}$	$6\overline{)30}$	$7\overline{)35}$	$6\overline{)6}$
$7\overline{)49}$	$6\overline{)42}$	$7\overline{)42}$	$6\overline{)0}$	$7\overline{)21}$
$6\overline{)18}$	$7\overline{)7}$	$6\overline{)36}$	$7\overline{)56}$	$6\overline{)24}$
$7\overline{)28}$	$6\overline{)48}$	$7\overline{)0}$	$6\overline{)12}$	$7\overline{)63}$
$4\overline{)16}$	$4\overline{)28}$	$5\overline{)20}$	$5\overline{)35}$	$4\overline{)36}$

28

Division: Checking the Answers

Directions: To check a division problem, multiply the quotient by the divisor. Add the remainder. The answer will be the dividend.

Example:

quotient $\begin{array}{r}58R1\\ 3\overline{)175}\\ -150\\ \hline 25\\ -24\\ \hline 1\end{array}$ $\begin{array}{r}58 \leftarrow \text{quotient}\\ \times 3 \leftarrow \text{divisor}\\ \hline 174\\ +1 \leftarrow \text{remainder}\\ \hline 175 \leftarrow \text{dividend}\end{array}$

divisor, dividend, remainder labels on left

Directions: Divide each problem, then draw a line from the division problem to the correct checking problem.

$\begin{array}{r}33\\ \times 7\end{array}$ $\begin{array}{r}53\\ \times 7\\ +2\end{array}$ $\begin{array}{r}97\\ \times 7\\ +3\end{array}$ $\begin{array}{r}135\\ \times 7\\ +1\end{array}$ $\begin{array}{r}113\\ \times 7\\ +1\end{array}$ $\begin{array}{r}119\\ \times 7\\ +1\end{array}$

$7\overline{)682}$ 97R3 $7\overline{)231}$ 33 $7\overline{)373}$ 53R2 $7\overline{)792}$ 113R1 $7\overline{)834}$ 119R1 $7\overline{)946}$ 135R1

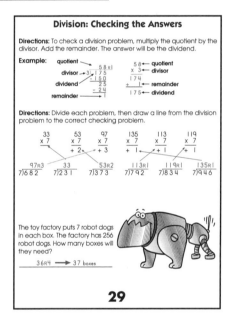

The toy factory puts 7 robot dogs in each box. The factory has 256 robot dogs. How many boxes will they need?

__36R4__ → 37 boxes

29

Division: Larger Numbers

Follow the steps for dividing larger numbers.

Example: Step 1: Divide the tens first. **Step 2:** Divide the ones next.

$3\overline{)66}$ $\begin{array}{r}2\\ 3\overline{)66}\\ -6\\ \hline 06\end{array}$ $\begin{array}{r}22\\ 3\overline{)66}\\ -6\\ \hline 06\\ -6\\ \hline 0\end{array}$

Directions: Divide.

$4\overline{)84}$ 21	$2\overline{)90}$ 45	$2\overline{)64}$ 32	$2\overline{)50}$ 25	$3\overline{)45}$ 15
$3\overline{)75}$ 25	$3\overline{)36}$ 12	$4\overline{)92}$ 23	$2\overline{)76}$ 38	$5\overline{)65}$ 13

In some larger numbers, the divisor goes into the first two digits of the dividend.

Example: $9\overline{)729}$ $\begin{array}{r}8\\ 9\overline{)729}\\ -72\\ \hline 09\end{array}$ $\begin{array}{r}81\\ 9\overline{)729}\\ -72\\ \hline 09\\ -9\\ \hline 0\end{array}$

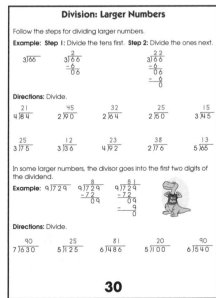

Directions: Divide.

$7\overline{)630}$ 90	$5\overline{)125}$ 25	$6\overline{)486}$ 81	$5\overline{)100}$ 20	$6\overline{)540}$ 90

30

Division: Two-Digit Divisors

Directions: Divide. Then check each answer on another sheet of paper by multiplying it by the divisor and adding the remainder.

Example: **Check:**

$\begin{array}{r}2\\ 12\overline{)256}\\ -24\\ \hline 1\end{array}$ $\begin{array}{r}21R4\\ 12\overline{)256}\\ -24\\ \hline 16\\ -12\\ \hline 4\end{array}$ $\begin{array}{r}21\\ \times 12\\ \hline 42\\ 210\\ \hline 252\\ +4\\ \hline 256\end{array}$

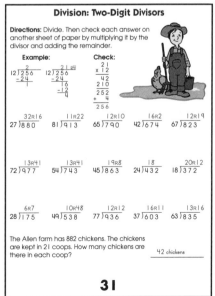

$27\overline{)880}$ 32R16	$81\overline{)913}$ 11R22	$65\overline{)790}$ 12R10	$42\overline{)674}$ 16R2	$67\overline{)823}$ 12R19
$72\overline{)977}$ 13R41	$54\overline{)743}$ 13R41	$45\overline{)863}$ 19R8	$24\overline{)432}$ 18	$18\overline{)372}$ 20R12
$28\overline{)175}$ 6R7	$49\overline{)538}$ 10R48	$77\overline{)936}$ 12R12	$37\overline{)603}$ 16R11	$63\overline{)835}$ 13R16

The Allen farm has 882 chickens. The chickens are kept in 21 coops. How many chickens are there in each coop?

__42 chickens__

31

Math: Grade 4

Averaging

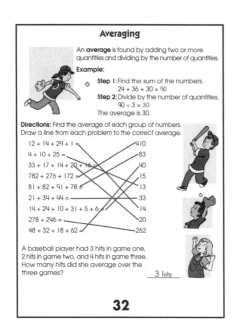

An **average** is found by adding two or more quantities and dividing by the number of quantities.

Example:

Step 1: Find the sum of the numbers.
24 + 36 + 30 = 90

Step 2: Divide by the number of quantities.
90 ÷ 3 = 30
The average is 30.

Directions: Find the average of each group of numbers. Draw a line from each problem to the correct average.

12 + 14 + 29 + 1 =   410
4 + 10 + 25 =   83
33 + 17 + 14 + 20 + 16 =   40
782 + 276 + 172 =   15
81 + 82 + 91 + 78 =   13
21 + 34 + 44 =   33
14 + 24 + 10 + 31 + 5 + 6 =   14
278 + 246 =   20
48 + 32 + 18 + 62 =   262

A baseball player had 3 hits in game one, 2 hits in game two, and 4 hits in game three. How many hits did she average over the three games?

3 hits

32

Geometry: Polygons

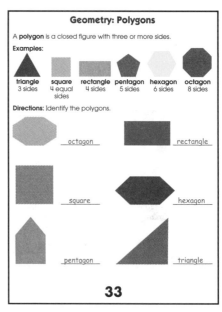

A **polygon** is a closed figure with three or more sides.

Examples:

triangle — 3 sides
square — 4 equal sides
rectangle — 4 sides
pentagon — 5 sides
hexagon — 6 sides
octagon — 8 sides

Directions: Identify the polygons.

octagon

rectangle

square

hexagon

pentagon

triangle

33

Geometry: Angles

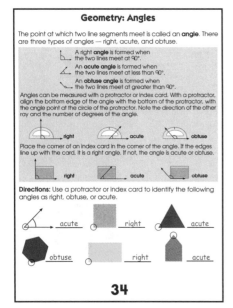

The point at which two line segments meet is called an **angle**. There are three types of angles — right, acute, and obtuse.

A right **angle** is formed when the two lines meet at 90°.
An **acute** angle is formed when the two lines meet at less than 90°.
An **obtuse** angle is formed when the two lines meet at greater than 90°.

Angles can be measured with a protractor or index card. With a protractor, align the bottom edge of the angle with the bottom of the protractor, with the angle point at the circle of the protractor. Note the direction of the other ray and the number of degrees of the angle.

right   acute   obtuse

Place the corner of an index card in the corner of the angle. If the edges line up with the card, it is a right angle. If not, the angle is acute or obtuse.

right   acute   obtuse

Directions: Use a protractor or index card to identify the following angles as right, obtuse, or acute.

acute   right   acute

obtuse   right   acute

34

Fractions

Directions: Name the fraction that is shaded.

Examples:

3 of 4 equal parts are shaded.

12 of 16 equal parts are shaded.

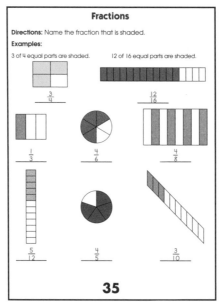

$\frac{3}{4}$

$\frac{12}{16}$

$\frac{1}{3}$

$\frac{4}{6}$

$\frac{4}{8}$

$\frac{5}{12}$

$\frac{4}{5}$

$\frac{3}{10}$

35

Working With Fractions

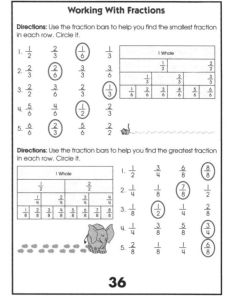

Directions: Use the fraction bars to help you find the smallest fraction in each row. Circle it.

1. $\frac{1}{2}$ $\frac{2}{3}$ ⓪$\frac{1}{6}$ $\frac{1}{3}$
2. $\frac{2}{3}$ ②$\frac{2}{6}$ $\frac{3}{6}$ $\frac{3}{3}$
3. $\frac{2}{2}$ $\frac{3}{6}$ $\frac{2}{3}$ ①$\frac{1}{3}$
4. $\frac{5}{6}$ $\frac{4}{6}$ ①$\frac{1}{2}$ $\frac{2}{3}$
5. $\frac{6}{6}$ ②$\frac{2}{3}$ $\frac{5}{6}$ $\frac{2}{2}$

1 Whole

Directions: Use the fraction bars to help you find the greatest fraction in each row. Circle it.

1. $\frac{1}{2}$ $\frac{3}{4}$ $\frac{6}{8}$ ⑧$\frac{8}{8}$
2. $\frac{1}{4}$ $\frac{1}{8}$ ⑦$\frac{7}{8}$ $\frac{1}{2}$
3. $\frac{1}{8}$ ①$\frac{1}{2}$ $\frac{1}{4}$ $\frac{2}{8}$
4. $\frac{1}{4}$ $\frac{3}{8}$ $\frac{5}{8}$ ③$\frac{3}{4}$
5. $\frac{2}{8}$ $\frac{1}{8}$ $\frac{1}{4}$ ⑥$\frac{6}{8}$

1 Whole

36

Equivalent Fractions

Equivalent fractions are two different fractions that represent the same number. **Example:** $\frac{1}{2}$ = $\frac{3}{6}$

Directions: Complete these equivalent fractions.

$\frac{1}{3} = \frac{2}{6}$ $\frac{1}{2} = \frac{2}{4}$ $\frac{3}{4} = \frac{6}{8}$ $\frac{1}{3} = \frac{3}{9}$

Directions: Circle the figures that show a fraction equivalent to figure A. Write the fraction for the shaded area under each figure.

A. $\frac{2}{4}$ B. $\frac{2}{8}$ C. $\frac{4}{16}$ D. $\frac{4}{8}$

E. $\frac{4}{4}$ F. $\frac{1}{4}$ G. $\frac{6}{8}$ H. $\frac{2}{4}$

To find an equivalent fraction, multiply both parts of the fraction by the same number.

Example: $\frac{2}{3} \times \frac{3}{3} = \frac{6}{9}$

Directions: Find an equivalent fraction.

$\frac{1}{4} = \frac{2}{8}$ $\frac{3}{4} = \frac{12}{16}$ $\frac{4}{5} = \frac{8}{10}$ $\frac{3}{8} = \frac{9}{24}$

37

Fractions: Addition

When adding fractions with the same denominator, the denominator stays the same. Add only the numerators.

Example: $\frac{\text{numerator}}{\text{denominator}}$ $\frac{1}{8} + \frac{2}{8} = \frac{3}{8}$

Directions: Add the fractions on the flowers. Begin in the center of each flower and add each petal. The first one is done for you.

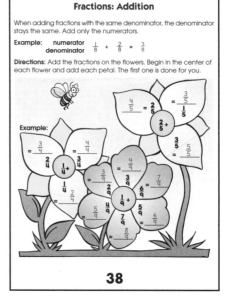

38

Fractions: Subtraction

When subtracting fractions with the same denominator, the denominator stays the same. Subtract only the numerators.

Directions: Solve the problems, working from left to right. As you find each answer, copy the letter from the key into the numbered blanks. The answer is the name of a famous American. The first one is done for you.

1. $\frac{3}{8} - \frac{2}{8} = \frac{1}{8}$

2. $\frac{2}{4} - \frac{1}{4} = \frac{1}{4}$

3. $\frac{5}{9} - \frac{3}{9} = \frac{2}{9}$

4. $\frac{2}{3} - \frac{1}{3} = \frac{1}{3}$

5. $\frac{8}{12} - \frac{7}{12} = \frac{1}{12}$

6. $\frac{4}{5} - \frac{1}{5} = \frac{3}{5}$

7. $\frac{6}{7} - \frac{3}{7} = \frac{3}{7}$

8. $\frac{4}{9} - \frac{1}{9} = \frac{3}{9}$

9. $\frac{11}{12} - \frac{7}{12} = \frac{4}{12}$

10. $\frac{7}{8} - \frac{3}{8} = \frac{4}{8}$

11. $\frac{4}{7} - \frac{2}{7} = \frac{2}{7}$

12. $\frac{14}{16} - \frac{7}{16} = \frac{7}{16}$

13. $\frac{18}{20} - \frac{13}{20} = \frac{5}{20}$

14. $\frac{14}{15} - \frac{3}{15} = \frac{11}{15}$

15. $\frac{5}{6} - \frac{3}{6} = \frac{2}{6}$

Key:

T $\frac{1}{8}$	P $\frac{5}{24}$	H $\frac{4}{4}$
F $\frac{4}{12}$	E $\frac{1}{9}$	J $\frac{3}{12}$
E $\frac{3}{6}$	O $\frac{2}{9}$	F $\frac{4}{8}$
R $\frac{7}{16}$	O $\frac{2}{8}$	Y $\frac{8}{20}$
Q $\frac{1}{32}$	M $\frac{1}{3}$	S $\frac{5}{20}$
A $\frac{1}{12}$	R $\frac{12}{15}$	S $\frac{3}{5}$
N $\frac{2}{6}$	O $\frac{11}{15}$	

Who helped write the Declaration of Independence?

T H O M A S   J E F F E R S O N
1 2 3 4 5 6   7 8 9 10 11 12 13 14 15

39

Reducing Fractions

Reducing a fraction means to find the greatest common factor and divide.

Example: $\frac{5}{15}$ factors of 5: 1, 5
factors of 15: 1, 3, 5, 15
$\frac{5 \div 5 = 1}{15 \div 5 = 3}$

5 is the greatest common factor. Divide both the numerator and denominator by 5.

Directions: Reduce each fraction. Circle the correct answer.

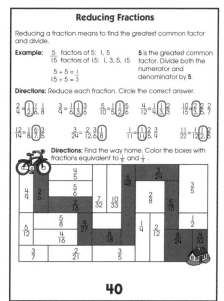

Directions: Find the way home. Color the boxes with fractions equivalent to $\frac{1}{8}$ and $\frac{1}{3}$.

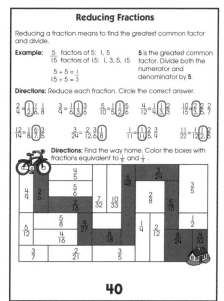

40

Fractions: Adding Mixed Numbers

When adding mixed numbers, add the fractions first, then the whole numbers.

Examples: $9\frac{1}{3} + 3\frac{1}{3} = 12\frac{2}{3}$ $2\frac{1}{8} + 1\frac{1}{8} = 3\frac{2}{8}$

Directions: Add the number in the center to the number in each surrounding section.

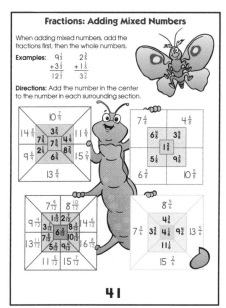

41

Fractions to Decimals

When a figure is divided into 10 equal parts, the parts are called **tenths**. Tenths can be written two ways—as a fraction or a decimal. A **decimal** is a number with one or more places to the right of a decimal point, such as 6.5 or 2.25. A **decimal point** is the dot between the ones place and the tenths place.

Examples:

ones	tenths
0	3

$\frac{3}{10}$ or 0.3 of the square is shaded.

$\frac{6}{10}$ 0.6

Directions: Write the decimal and fraction for the shaded parts of the following figures.

$\frac{3}{10}$ 0.3 $\frac{9}{10}$ 0.9 $1\frac{5}{10}$ 1.5

$1\frac{8}{10}$ 1.8 $\frac{4}{10}$ 0.4 $\frac{8}{10}$ 0.8

42

Decimals

Directions: Add or subtract. Remember to include the decimal point in your answers.

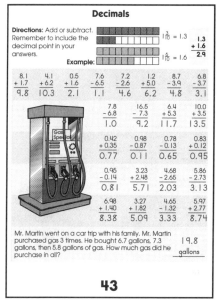

$1\frac{3}{10} = 1.3$
$1\frac{6}{10} = 1.6$

$\begin{array}{r} 1.3 \\ +1.6 \\ \hline 2.9 \end{array}$

Example:

$\begin{array}{r}8.1\\+1.7\\\hline 9.8\end{array}$	$\begin{array}{r}4.1\\+6.2\\\hline 10.3\end{array}$	$\begin{array}{r}0.5\\+1.6\\\hline 2.1\end{array}$	$\begin{array}{r}7.6\\-6.5\\\hline 1.1\end{array}$	$\begin{array}{r}7.2\\-2.6\\\hline 4.6\end{array}$	$\begin{array}{r}1.2\\+5.0\\\hline 6.2\end{array}$	$\begin{array}{r}8.7\\-3.9\\\hline 4.8\end{array}$	$\begin{array}{r}6.8\\-3.7\\\hline 3.1\end{array}$

$\begin{array}{r}7.8\\-6.8\\\hline 1.0\end{array}$ $\begin{array}{r}16.5\\-7.3\\\hline 9.2\end{array}$ $\begin{array}{r}6.4\\+5.3\\\hline 11.7\end{array}$ $\begin{array}{r}10.0\\+3.5\\\hline 13.5\end{array}$

$\begin{array}{r}0.42\\+0.35\\\hline 0.77\end{array}$ $\begin{array}{r}0.98\\-0.87\\\hline 0.11\end{array}$ $\begin{array}{r}0.78\\-0.13\\\hline 0.65\end{array}$ $\begin{array}{r}0.83\\+0.12\\\hline 0.95\end{array}$

$\begin{array}{r}0.95\\-0.14\\\hline 0.81\end{array}$ $\begin{array}{r}3.23\\+2.48\\\hline 5.71\end{array}$ $\begin{array}{r}4.68\\-2.65\\\hline 2.03\end{array}$ $\begin{array}{r}5.86\\-2.73\\\hline 3.13\end{array}$

$\begin{array}{r}6.98\\+1.40\\\hline 8.38\end{array}$ $\begin{array}{r}3.27\\+1.82\\\hline 5.09\end{array}$ $\begin{array}{r}4.65\\-1.32\\\hline 3.33\end{array}$ $\begin{array}{r}5.97\\+2.77\\\hline 8.74\end{array}$

Mr. Martin went on a car trip with his family. Mr. Martin purchased gas 3 times. He bought 6.7 gallons, 7.3 gallons, then 5.8 gallons of gas. How much gas did he purchase in all?

19.8 gallons

43

Decimals: Hundredths

The next smallest decimal unit after a tenth is called a **hundredth**. One hundredth is one unit of a figure divided into 100 units. Written as a decimal, it is one digit to the right of the tenths place.

Example:

One square divided into hundredths, 34 hundredths are shaded. Write: 0.34.

ones	tenths	hundredths
0	3	4

0.34

Directions: Write the decimal for the shaded parts of the following figures.

0.24   0.50   0.53   0.05

1.48   1.10

44

Graphing

A **graph** is a drawing that shows information about changes in numbers.

Directions: Answer the questions by reading the graphs.

Bar Graph

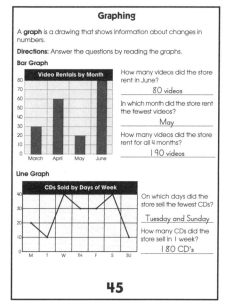

Video Rentals by Month

How many videos did the store rent in June?

80 videos

In which month did the store rent the fewest videos?

May

How many videos did the store rent for all 4 months?

190 videos

Line Graph

CDs Sold by Days of Week

On which days did the store sell the fewest CDs?

Tuesday and Sunday

How many CDs did the store sell in 1 week?

180 CD's

45

Math: Grade 4

Guess the Color

Probability shows the chance that a given event will happen. To show probability, write a fraction. The number of different possibilities is the denominator. The number of times the event could happen is the numerator. (Remember to reduce fractions to the lowest terms.)

Directions: Look at the spinner. What is the probability that the arrow will land on . . .

1. red? $\frac{3}{8}$
2. blue? $\frac{2}{8} = \frac{1}{4}$
3. yellow? $\frac{1}{8}$
4. green? $\frac{1}{8}$
5. orange? $\frac{1}{8}$

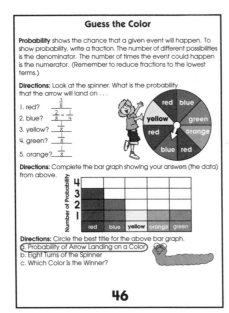

Directions: Complete the bar graph showing your answers (the data) from above.

Number of Probability
4
3
2
1

red | blue | yellow | orange | green

Directions: Circle the best title for the above bar graph.
a. Probability of Arrow Landing on a Color
b. Eight Turns of the Spinner
c. Which Color Is the Winner?

46

Graphing: Finding Ordered Pairs

Graphs or grids are sometimes used to find the location of objects.

Example: The ice-cream cone is located at point (5, 6) on the graph. To find the ice cream's location, follow the line to the bottom of the grid to get the first number — 5. Then go back to the ice cream and follow the grid line to the left for the second number — 6.

Directions: Write the ordered pair for the following objects. The first one is done for you.

book (4, 8)   bike (8,6)   suitcase (1,4)   house (8,3)
globe (4,4)   cup (9,9)   triangle (7,2)   airplane (7,8)

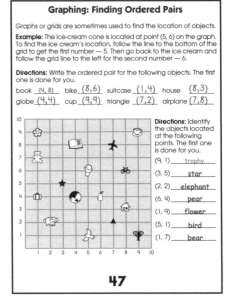

Directions: Identify the objects located at the following points. The first one is done for you.

(9, 1)   trophy
(3, 5)   star
(2, 2)   elephant
(6, 4)   pear
(1, 9)   flower
(5, 1)   bird
(1, 7)   bear

47

Probability

Another thinking skill to get your brain in gear is figuring probability. Probability is the likelihood or chance that something will happen. Probability is expressed and written as a ratio.

The probability of tossing heads or tails on a coin is one in two (1:2).

The probability of rolling any number on a die is one in six (1:6).

The probability of getting a red on this spinner is two in four (2:4).

The probability of drawing an ace from a deck of cards is four in fifty-two (4:52).

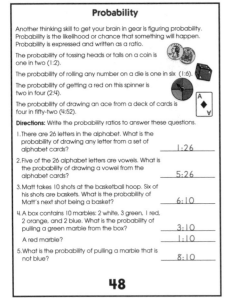

Directions: Write the probability ratios to answer these questions.

1. There are 26 letters in the alphabet. What is the probability of drawing any letter from a set of alphabet cards?   1:26

2. Five of the 26 alphabet letters are vowels. What is the probability of drawing a vowel from the alphabet cards?   5:26

3. Matt takes 10 shots at the basketball hoop. Six of his shots are baskets. What is the probability of Matt's next shot being a basket?   6:10

4. A box contains 10 marbles: 2 white, 3 green, 1 red, 2 orange, and 2 blue. What is the probability of pulling a green marble from the box?   3:10

   A red marble?   1:10

5. What is the probability of pulling a marble that is not blue?   8:10

48

How Many Outfits?

Directions: Suppose you had two pairs of jeans (one blue and the other gray) and three shirts (orange, red, and green). How many different outfits could you wear? Use a tree diagram to help you with the answer.

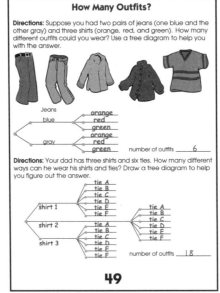

Jeans
blue — orange / red / green
gray — orange / red / green

number of outfits   6

Directions: Your dad has three shirts and six ties. How many different ways can he wear his shirts and ties? Draw a tree diagram to help you figure out the answer.

shirt 1 — tie A / tie B / tie C / tie D / tie E / tie F
shirt 2 — tie A / tie B / tie C / tie D / tie E / tie F
shirt 3 — tie A / tie B / tie C / tie D / tie E / tie F

number of outfits   18

49

Measurement: Fractions of an Inch

An inch is divided into smaller units, or fractions, of an inch.

Example: This stick of gum is $2\frac{3}{8}$ inches long.

Chewing Gum

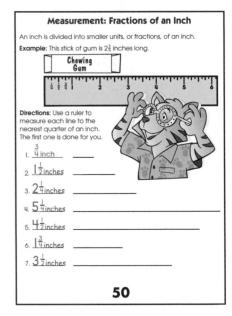

Directions: Use a ruler to measure each line to the nearest quarter of an inch. The first one is done for you.

1. $\frac{3}{4}$ inch _____
2. $1\frac{1}{2}$ inches _____
3. $2\frac{1}{4}$ inches _____
4. $5\frac{1}{4}$ inches _____
5. $4\frac{1}{2}$ inches _____
6. $1\frac{3}{4}$ inches _____
7. $3\frac{1}{2}$ inches _____

50

½ Inch

½ inch or ⅟₂ in.

The stick is 2½ inches long.

2½ is read
two and one half.

inches | 1 | 2 | 3 | 4

The nail is __3½__ inches long.

Directions: Find the length of each picture to the nearest ½ inch.

1. __1½__ in.
2. __2½__ in.
3. __1__ in.
4. __3½__ in.
5. __4½__ in.
6. __3__ in.

Directions: Use a ruler to draw a line segment for each measurement.

7. 1½ in.
8. 3½ in.   7–10. Have a parent or teacher check your work.
9. 4½ in.
10. 5 in.

51

Measurement: Foot, Yard, Mile

Directions: Choose the measure of distance you would use for each object.

1 foot = 12 inches
1 yard = 3 feet
1 mile = 1,760 yards or 5,280 feet

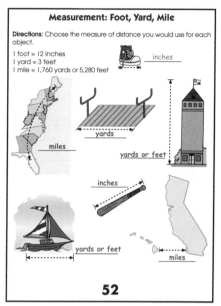

inches

yards

miles

yards or feet

inches

yards or feet

miles

52

Metric Measurement: Centimeter, Meter, Kilometer

In the metric system, there are three units of linear measurement: centimeter (cm), meter (m), and kilometer (km).

Centimeters (cm) are used to measure the lengths of small to medium-sized objects. **Meters (m)** measure the lengths of longer objects, such as the width of a swimming pool or height of a tree (100 cm = 1 meter). **Kilometers (km)** measure long distances, such as the distance from Cleveland to Cincinnati or the width of the Atlantic Ocean (1,000 m = 1 km).

Directions: Write whether you would use cm, m, or km to measure each object.

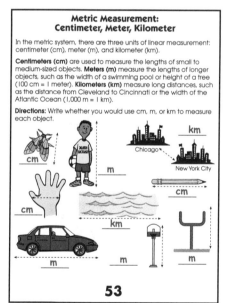

cm

km

Chicago

km

New York City

m

cm

cm

km

m

m

m

53

Millimeter

1 millimeter (mm)

1 centimeter (cm)

1 centimeter = 10 millimeters
1 cm = 10 mm

Line segment CD is __7__ centimeters or __70__ millimeters long.

Directions: Solve the problems. Find the length of each line segment to the nearest centimeter. Then, find the length of each line segment to the nearest millimeter.

1. __7__ cm   __70__ mm
2. __4__ cm   __40__ mm
3. __5__ cm   __50__ mm
4. __3__ cm   __30__ mm

Find the length of each line segment to the nearest millimeter.

5. __64__ mm
6. __45__ mm
7. __73__ mm
8. __42__ mm

Use a ruler to draw a line segment for each measurement.

9. 50 mm
10. 80 mm
11. 25 mm   9–12. Have a parent or teacher check your work.
12. 55 mm

54

Units of Length

25 cm = ? mm	18 m = ? cm	9 m = ? mm	7 km = ? m
1 cm = 10 mm	1 m = 100 cm	1 m = 1000 mm	1 km = 1000 m
×10	×100	×1000	×1000
×25 / 250	×18 / 1800	×9 / 9000	×7 / 7000
25 cm = 250 mm	18 m = 1800 cm	9 m = mm	7 km = m

Directions: Complete the following.

9 cm = __90__ mm   7 cm = __70__ mm

9 m = __900__ cm   6 m = __600__ cm

9 m = __9000__ mm   4 m = __4000__ mm

9 km = __9000__ m   5 km = __5000__ m

16 m = __1600__ cm   8 m = __8000__ mm

89 km = __89000__ m   46 m = __4600__ mm

28 cm = __280__ mm   18 km = __18000__ m

13 m = __13000__ mm   42 cm = __420__ mm

16 m = __16000__ mm   10 m = __1000__ cm

10 km = __10000__ m   25 m = __25000__ mm

55

Measurement: Perimeter and Area

Perimeter is the distance around a figure. It is found by adding the lengths of the sides. **Area** is the number of square units needed to cover a region. The area is found by adding the number of square units. A unit can be any unit of measure. Most often, inches, feet, or yards are used.

Directions: Find the perimeter and area for each figure. The first one is done for you.   ☐ = 1 square unit

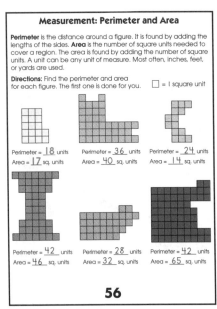

Perimeter = 18 units
Area = 17 sq. units

Perimeter = 36 units
Area = 40 sq. units

Perimeter = 24 units
Area = 14 sq. units

Perimeter = 42 units
Area = 46 sq. units

Perimeter = 28 units
Area = 32 sq. units

Perimeter = 42 units
Area = 65 sq. units

56

Perimeter

The distance around a figure is called its **perimeter**.

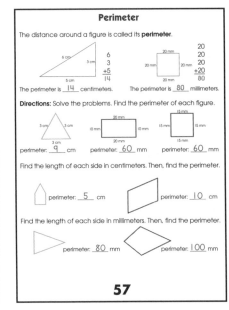

The perimeter is 14 centimeters.

The perimeter is 80 millimeters.

Directions: Solve the problems. Find the perimeter of each figure.

perimeter: 9 cm

perimeter: 60 mm

perimeter: 60 mm

Find the length of each side in centimeters. Then, find the perimeter.

perimeter: 5 cm

perimeter: 10 cm

Find the length of each side in millimeters. Then, find the perimeter.

perimeter: 80 mm

perimeter: 100 mm

57

Measurement: Volume

Volume is the number of cubic units that fit inside a figure.

Directions: Find the volume of each figure. The first one is done for you.

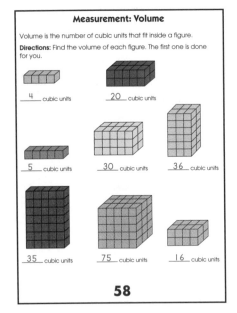

4 cubic units

20 cubic units

5 cubic units

30 cubic units

36 cubic units

35 cubic units

75 cubic units

16 cubic units

58

Measurement: Volume

The volume of a figure can also be calculated by multiplying the length times the width times the height.
Use the formula: V= l x w x h.

Example:

3 x 5 x 2 = 30 cubic feet

Directions: Find the volume of the following figures. Label your answers in cubic feet, inches, or yards. The first one is done for you.

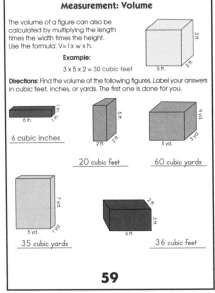

6 cubic inches

20 cubic feet

60 cubic yards

35 cubic yards

36 cubic feet

59

Measurement: Ounce, Pound, Ton

The **ounce**, **pound**, and **ton** are units in the standard system for measuring weight.

Directions: Choose the measure of weight you would use for each object.

16 ounces = 1 pound
2,000 pounds = 1 ton

ounce   pound   ton

Example:

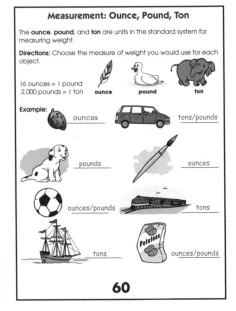

ounces

tons/pounds

pounds

ounces

ounces/pounds

tons

tons

ounces/pounds

60

Metric Measurement: Gram and Kilogram

Grams and **kilograms** are measurements of weight in the metric system. A gram (g) weighs about ⅟₂₈ of an ounce. A grape or paper clip weighs about one gram. There are 1,000 grams in a kilogram. A kilogram (kg) weighs about 2.2 pounds. A brick weighs about 1 kilogram.

Directions: Choose grams or kilograms to measure the following.

Example:

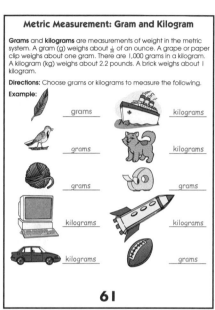

grams	kilograms
grams	kilograms
grams	grams
kilograms	kilograms
kilograms	grams

61

Time Problems

Directions: Draw the hands on the clocks to show the starting time and the ending time. Then, write the answer to the question.

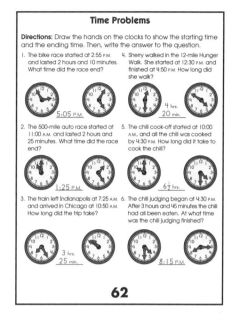

1. The bike race started at 2:55 P.M. and lasted 2 hours and 10 minutes. What time did the race end?
__5:05 P.M.__

2. The 500-mile auto race started at 11:00 A.M. and lasted 2 hours and 25 minutes. What time did the race end?
__1:25 P.M.__

3. The train left Indianapolis at 7:25 A.M. and arrived in Chicago at 10:50 A.M. How long did the trip take?
__3 hrs. 25 min.__

4. Sherry walked in the 12-mile Hunger Walk. She started at 12:30 P.M. and finished at 4:50 P.M. How long did she walk?
__4 hrs. 20 min.__

5. The chili cook-off started at 10:00 A.M., and all the chili was cooked by 4:30 P.M. How long did it take to cook the chili?
__6½ hrs.__

6. The chili judging began at 4:30 P.M. After 3 hours and 45 minutes the chili had all been eaten. At what time was the chili judging finished?
__8:15 P.M.__

62

Money

I cent = 1¢ or $0.01	I dollar = $1.00
3 cents = __3¢__ or __$0.03__	3 dollars and 2 cents = __$3.02__
65 cents = __65¢__ or __$0.65__	4 dollars and 59 cents = __$4.59__
6 cents = __6¢__ or $ __0.06__	6 dollars and 3 cents = __$6.03__
98 cents = __98¢__ or $ __0.98__	5 dollars and 72 cents = __$5.72__

Directions: Complete the following.

5 cents = __5__ ¢	25¢ = $ __.25__	$0.83 = __83__ ¢
10 cents = $ __.10__	50¢ = $ __.50__	$0.04 = __4__ ¢
25 cents = __25__ ¢	75¢ = $ __.75__	$0.29 = __29__ ¢
50 cents = $ __.50__	10¢ = $ __.10__	$0.06 = __6__ ¢
85 cents = __85__ ¢	95¢ = $ __.95__	$0.60 = __60__ ¢
100 cents = $ __1.00__	5¢ = $ __.05__	$0.99 = __99__ ¢

Directions: Complete the following.

4 dollars and 8 cents = $ __4.08__
7 dollars and 63 cents = $ __7.63__
3 dollars and 9 cents = $ __3.09__
6 dollars and 19 cents = $ __6.19__
5 dollars and 79 cents = $ __5.79__
18 dollars and 75 cents = $ __18.75__
$6.25 = 6 dollars and __25__ cents
$3.75 = __3__ dollars and 75 cents
$7.05 = 7 dollars and __5__ cents
$9.65 = __9__ dollars and 65 cents
$4.19 = __4__ dollars and __19__ cents
$8.69 = __8__ dollars and __69__ cents

63

Money

Add the numbers.

```
 25¢      $0.85
 45¢       2.08
+19¢      +3.76
 89¢      $6.69
```

Subtract the numbers.

```
 72¢      $12.07
-26¢       -4.83
 46¢       $7.24
```

Write ¢ or $ and a decimal point in the answer.

Write ¢ or $ and a decimal point in the answer.

Directions: Add or subtract.

```
  23¢       47¢      $0.46      $5.47     $36.95
 +44¢      +25¢      +0.73      +8.21     +72.02
  67¢       72¢      $1.19     $13.68    $108.97

  79¢       56¢      $1.27      $4.67     $36.78
 -23¢      -27¢      -0.53      -2.89     -27.90
  56¢       29¢      $ .74      $1.78      $ 8.88

  14¢        6¢      $0.57      $5.25     $16.96
 +71¢      +87¢      +0.68      +9.46     +27.45
  85¢       93¢      $1.25     $14.71     $44.41

  88¢       92¢      $2.64      $6.27     $49.78
 -69¢      -89¢      -0.57      -2.89     -18.89
  19¢        3¢      $2.07      $3.38     $30.89

  12¢       43¢      $0.75      $0.12     $47.52
  39¢       27¢       0.65       4.69      89.25
 +24¢      +26¢      +0.97      +5.87     +67.47
  75¢       96¢      $2.37     $10.68    $204.24

 $2.46     $1.57     $3.07      $7.00     $60.47
 -0.87     -0.99     -1.85      -2.48     -27.59
 $1.59     $ .58     $1.22      $4.52     $32.88
```

64

Fast Food

Mealwormy is the latest restaurant of that famous fast food creator, Buggs I. Lyke. His Mealwormy Burger costs $1.69 for the regular size and $0.79 for the larger size. A Cricket Cola is $0.89.

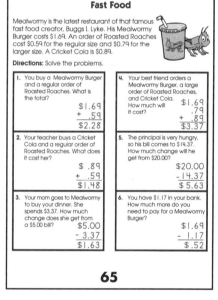

Directions: Solve the problems.

1. You buy a Mealwormy Hunger Burger and a regular order of Roasted Roaches. What is the total?
```
 $1.69
  +.59
 $2.28
```

2. Your teacher buys a Cricket Cola and a regular order of Roasted Roaches. What does it cost her?
```
 $ .89
  +.59
 $1.48
```

3. Your mom goes to Mealwormy to buy your dinner. She spends $3.37. How much change does she get from a $5.00 bill?
```
 $5.00
 -3.37
 $1.63
```

4. Your best friend orders a Mealwormy Burger, a large order of Roasted Roaches, and Cricket Cola. How much will it cost?
```
 $1.69
   .79
  +.89
 $3.37
```

5. The principal is very hungry, so his bill comes to $14.37. How much change will he get from $20.00?
```
 $20.00
 -14.37
 $ 5.63
```

6. You have $1.17 in your bank. How much more do you need to pay for a Mealwormy Burger?
```
 $1.69
 -1.17
 $ .52
```

65

Multiplying Money

Money is multiplied in the same way other numbers are. The only difference is a dollar sign and a decimal point are added to the final product.

Directions: Follow the steps, then multiply these problems.

Steps:

1. Multiply by ones.
   1. 4 x 8 = 32 (Carry the 3.)
   2. 4 x 2 = 8 + 3 = 11 (Carry the 1.)
   3. 4 x 4 = 16 + 1 = 17

```
      1 3
   $4.28        $3.42        $5.42
   x  34        x  25        x  61
   1712
              $85.50       $330.62
```

2. 1. Cross out the carried digits.
   2. Add the zero.

```
      XX
   $4.28
   x  34
   1712
       0
```

3. Multiply by tens.
   1. 3 x 8 = 24 (Carry the 2.)
   2. 3 x 2 = 6 + 2 = 8
   3. 3 x 4 = 12

```
        2
   $4.28
   x  34
   1712
  12840
```
```
   $3.81        $8.20
   x  46        x  55

  $175.26      $451.00
```

```
   $4.28
   x  34
   1712
```

4. Add.
   1,712 + 12,840 = 14,552

```
   $4.28
   x  34
   1712
  +12840
   14,552
```

5. Add the dollar sign and the decimal point.

```
   $4.28
   x  34
   1712
  +12840
  $145.52
```
```
   $9.42        $4.23
   x  31        x  96

  $292.02      $406.08
```

66

Money Math

Directions: Solve these problems. Remember the decimal point and dollar sign in your answers.

```
  $3.42    $2.45    $6.42    $8.43
  x  27    x  34    x  56    x  30
 $92.34   $83.30  $359.52  $252.90


  $0.49    $2.53    $8.21    $4.21
  x  56    x  41    x  37    x  36
 $27.44  $103.73  $303.77  $151.56


  $5.41    $0.21    $0.89    $4.25
  x  42    x  84    x  32    x  31
$227.22   $17.64   $28.48  $131.75
```

67

Too Much Information

Directions: Cross out the information not needed and solve the problems.

4. Six of the students spent a total of $16.50 for refreshments and $21.00 for their tickets. How much did each spend for refreshments?

$2.75

1. All 20 of the students from Sandy's class went to the movies. Tickets cost $3.50 each. Drinks cost $0.95 each. How much altogether did the students spend on tickets?

$70.00

5. Of the students, 11 were girls and 9 were boys. At $1.50 per ticket, how much did the boys' tickets cost altogether?

$13.50

2. Five students had ice cream, 12 others had candy. Ice cream cost $0.75 per cup. How much did the students spend on ice cream?

$3.75

6. Mary paid $0.95 for an orange drink and $0.65 for a candy bar. Sarah paid $2.50 for popcorn. How much did Mary's refreshments cost her?

$1.60

3. Seven of the 20 students did not like the movie. Three of the 20 students had seen the movie before. How many students had not seen the movie before?

17 students

7. Ten of the students went back to see the movie again the next day. Each student paid $3.50 for a ticket, $2.50 for popcorn, and $0.95 for a soft drink. How much did each student pay?

$6.95

68

Perplexing Problems

Directions: Solve these problems.

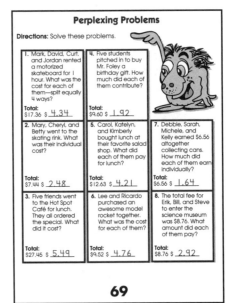

1. Mark, David, Curt, and Jordan rented a motorized skateboard for 1 hour. What was the cost for each of them—split equally 4 ways?

Total: $17.36 $4.34

4. Five students pitched in to buy Mr. Foley a birthday gift. How much did each of them contribute?

Total: $9.60 $1.92

2. Mary, Cheryl, and Betty went to the skating rink. What was their individual cost?

Total: $7.44 $2.48

5. Carol, Katelyn, and Kimberly bought lunch at their favorite salad shop. What did each of them pay for lunch?

Total: $12.63 $4.21

7. Debbie, Sarah, Michele, and Kelly earned $6.56 altogether collecting cans. How much did each of them earn individually?

Total: $6.56 $1.64

3. Five friends went to the Hot Spot Café for lunch. They all ordered the special. What did it cost?

Total: $27.45 $5.49

6. Lee and Ricardo purchased an awesome model rocket together. What was the cost for each of them?

Total: $9.52 $4.76

8. The total fee for Erik, Bill, and Steve to enter the science museum was $8.76. What amount did each of them pay?

Total: $8.76 $2.92

69
